A Southern Season

Rural Stories

MICHAEL K. BRANTLEY

Black Rose Writing | Texas

ISBN: 978-1-68513-141-8
PUBLISHED BY BLACK ROSE WRITING
www.blackrosewriting.com

Printed in the United States of America
Suggested Retail Price (SRP) $19.95

A Southern Season is printed in Garamond Premier Pro

*As a planet-friendly publisher, Black Rose Writing does its best to eliminate unnecessary waste to reduce paper usage and energy costs, while never compromising the reading experience. As a result, the final word count vs. page count may not meet common expectations.

Other Books by Michael K. Brantley

Memory Cards: Portraits from a Rural Journey

Galvanized: The Odyssey of a Reluctant Carolina Confederate

It's a Time in the Land: The Best of the Soap Box

This book is dedicated to
Jim, Emily, Jon, Rebecca, Alex, Luke, and Liza

Thanks for equipping me with the tools I use every time I write.

Acknowledgments

Many thanks to Reagan Rothe at Black Rose for believing in another project of mine, and to David King for always outstanding design.

Many thanks to authors Liza Wieland and Thomas Ford Conlan for reading and offering comments on this book. It takes time and energy and I appreciate both.

As always, my first and most patient reader, Kristi Brantley, always gives me good guidance and it is hard to place a value on that.

A version of some of these chapters appeared in literary journals and for that I'm grateful and proud to be associated with them. "Cooking Collards" and "No More to the Lake" were published in *The Broad River Review*; "Those Old Barns" in *daCunha* (UK); "Homegrown Tomatoes" and "Homeplace" in *museum of americana*; "Shopping List, 1937" in *Parhelion Literary Magazine*; "Number One Pork Chop Man" and "Memory Cards" in *The Magnolia Review*.

A Southern Season

Contents

1
Cooking Collards

Last fall after the first frost, I called my mama and asked if she would help me cook some collards. I knew she would tell me to come on over, but since the greens aren't her favorite, I thought I should at least try to sweeten the pot a little and make it sound adventurous, if the collard can be such.

"I want to do it old style, and I'm not talking about common collards, I'm talking about cabbage-collards," I said. I may or may not have mentioned that I also did not have a stockpot large enough, or as she would say, seasoned enough, for cooking those big, leafy, stereotypical Southern-staple greens. Mama taught me the way around a kitchen from the time I was old enough to see over the stovetop. Back then it was a performance every night, squash and onions in one pan, cucumbers and tomatoes sloshing in vinegar in a ceramic bowl, and just the right amount of seasonings to keep the harmonies tight. I miss those times more as the cooler days begin to signal year's end.

With the help of another first-rate cook, my sister, Jane, I sourced a couple of shapely, robust heads and drove over to Mama's on a cool Saturday afternoon. After a little prep work on the back steps, I brought them inside, greeted at the door by the familiar smells of my childhood. Traces of something baked and chocolate always lingered in the long, dark, hallway leading into the main part of the house, up to the kitchen on the left. A generation before, Mama would have been in the groove she'd worn in the linoleum floor, flitting her small, energy-packed frame between the oven, the sink and the table, mixing something, chopping something, stirring something, so there would always be plenty to eat for whoever might drop by, be it me, my siblings, or the preacher.

We pulled the loose, light green leaves apart, and washed them over and over in the large, stainless steel sink, and then I took them to an old oak cutting board to trim away the bitter center stem, as advised by Jane. This seemed strange to Mama. Her mother did not permit waste. Granny had suffered through the Depression, and then widowhood the last fifty years of her life. Long after the hardest of times, Granny still served every part of a chicken on her table, including the feet. In her eyes, removing collard stems would have marked me as not having good sense.

That worn and tarnished silver pot with the black bottom, the starting point of countless meals of chicken pastry, and the blanching of thousands of vegetables prior to canning or freezing, had been retired. Mama informed me that it sprung a leak some time back, but in a nod to Granny's ways of re-purposing, she of course had not disposed of it. It was now used to transport vegetables from her small box of plantings, the evolution of time and age and practicality from our farm days passed.

Ironically, Mama upgraded to a stylish Paula Deen model, an ample, if slightly undersized replacement. We considered using the traditional ham bone or sausage as seasoning, but decided against it since we had a vegetarian and others with dietary restrictions in the family. Instead, we opted for extra virgin olive oil, and homegrown dried and crushed red pepper. We didn't even use the collards I remembered growing up with, those that varied from dark green to darker green, bitter smelling even when fresh, and downright foul, almost sulfur-smelling when cooked and chopped into mush.

No, these were the poor man's-gone-chic-cabbage collards, grown from closely guarded seeds, so valuable as to be included in some farmers' wills. With a tantalizingly sweet aroma, they offered a smooth taste, and required very little table seasoning. It was a dish even a non-collard eater could appreciate, something expected from a cook with some sense.

• • •

"Go out to the smokehouse and get me an armful of new potatoes."

This was a common order directed at me, from when I was a young boy until I left the house after college. Often, other directives would follow such as, "And then go back to the freezer and get a bag of corn" or "Bring a jar of squash and some snaps from the pantry." Sometimes I was sent to get a country ham, put it gently in the boot of Mama's car and ride with her to town so she could get the butcher to carve perfect slices for supper.

The butcher shop was cold and smelled funny, but meant my favorite meals were on the way. The only conflict was thick versus thin slices, as our house was divided. Ever the blessed peacekeeper, Mama directed the counter man. She and I were firmly in the thin camp, and we were the ones doing the dirty work of getting the ham there, so it appeared the scales of equality tipped ever so slightly in our favor.

Our first smokehouse was an old shack that was a holdover from the previous owners of my parents' farm, and its tar paper-and-shingle appearance hinted it was the last place anyone would want to store food. The shed tilted towards the field away from the house, not by design, but by evolution. Myths alleged by my older brothers asserted that many varieties of deadly snakes and other exotic creatures lived in the deep shadows. Whenever and wherever those two found a snakeskin, they'd be sure to place it in plain sight, near whatever they knew Mama might send me after.

Smokehouses were standard in our rural county, even in the 1980s. We cured hams and sausage and stored potatoes; others did the same, but some left space for corn liquor and the occasional still. When my folks finally got around to a remodel, they had the old outbuilding torn down. From that pile a sturdy modern replacement arose that included a smokehouse in the back, complete with worktables, shelves, and hooks for hams. There was even a drain in the concrete floor for easy cleanup.

I could be critical of Daddy when I was a child, but the man knew how to make sausage and cure a ham. I never remember one going bad, which was always a risk. Other than a brief flirtation with brown sugar curing, Daddy always preferred working with salt. His touch was deft, hams were never over seasoned, never bland, instead, just right, tender and ready for that old black cast iron frying pan. It's been decades since he worked that magic, but his recipes remain in pencil, sketched on the unpainted wall, this much salt, that much pepper. The sausage was savory, several links done mild, others hot with red pepper, with just enough sage. Some local labels make a fine product, but nothing tastes quite like home, a flavor long gone from an empty curing room, but the aroma still lingering.

• • •

As we minded the collard pot, peeking too often, I asked Mama if she remembered how often we used to have country ham, and how it was our version of a steak dinner.

"What's country ham?" she asked me dryly. "We haven't had that since Buck was a calf," another expression she often used. "Can you even buy it anymore, other than that mess in the plastic packs?" She was referring to the tough, sinewy, vacuum-packed lumps of unknown provenance tossed on tables near the meat section in chain stores.

Country ham was in regular rotation on our supper table, with plenty of vegetables. We never thought it to be a delicacy, or that one day we wouldn't have it. Good country ham is hard to find now, and I can find countless articles listing it as yet another villain in the lineup of deadly Southern victuals.

A few weeks after that conversation, I found a church booth at the State Fair serving homemade biscuits with country ham. At two dollars, it was worth the gamble, and they handed me a hot, moist, pouch of fluffy goodness, warm to the touch, stuffed with two just-right, thin slices of country ham. The only thing it was missing was a dab of Duke's mayonnaise, and maybe a thick hunk of too-orange hoop cheese. I sat down on a bench and let my mouth savor the memory, a trip back to another time, a taste of the past. It was divine.

• • •

I did not grow up loving collards, because we didn't have them often. It makes sense that the kitchen serves the preference of the cook. After all, who wants to stand over a reeking pot of greens, in a house with no central air, cooking a dish that very often might be paired with a main course of hog chitlins? My daddy liked collards, and every once in a while, Mama would relent and make dog bread, hominy, collards and chitlins. Dog bread can come in many variations, but at our house it was cornmeal and water mixed and squashed into a baking pan and oven cooked to a crunchy crust. Mama and I would pick out the sausage or ham used to flavor the greens, or she'd throw a couple of pieces of cubed steak in a pan, as neither of us could negotiate the consumption of hog intestines.

Even with seasoning, the collards were often bitter (or "earthy" as critics on TV like to say), but still better than turnip or mustard greens. It all looked like weeds to me when pulverized for the table and could only be dealt with by generous amounts or vinegar, red pepper or Mama's homemade sweet pepper and onion relish. A quarter inch layer could make anything edible that was supposed to be good for you.

•   •   •

I developed a taste for collards because my sister once decided it was the one thing she hadn't attempted to master. She's never revealed much about that culinary journey, but she figured it out by slipping them onto the menu of a family gathering one year. Soon she was bringing them to our immense family Thanksgiving meal at my parents' house, before eventually taking over the entire operation in the 1990s.

While I really wanted some collards last fall, I mostly wanted to cook with Mama again, just the two of us in her kitchen, like it was after my brothers and sisters had all married and moved out, and she showed me how to coax palatable miracles out of whatever was on hand. I asked a lot of questions, and Mama had answers for all of them. Her wisdom and patience always extended beyond how to make a snap bean casserole or fry okra.

The tools in her kitchen, which I took for granted until I too moved out and started my own kitchen with my wife, were relics that knew the recipes by heart. A cast-iron frying pan, solid black from generations of use, was used for everything from country ham, to hamburger steak, to fried chicken, corn fritters and fried green tomatoes. Ceramic mixing bowls, an old-time tin sifter, a couple of weathered butcher knives and a variety of wooden spoons did the yeoman's work.

Mama seemed excited, too. By the time the afternoon was over, the best tasting dish served was the conversation, the memories, the aroma of good times past that neither of us knew then would be such a delicacy now.

• • •

As the afternoon wore on, Mama and I considered the foods fading not just from our family's tables, but from existence. Why didn't anybody make apple jacks anymore? Had anyone written down the recipe for her sliced sweet potato pie, in both lemon and spice versions? How about those passed down things like tea cookies, homemade peach ice cream, sourdough bread, cinnamon rolls, blackberry cobbler, and chicken pastry? Did the grandchildren know how to make the family barbecue sauce?

The same pot I had hoped to cook the collards in was the one Mama used for chicken pastry. "It ain't nothing to it," Mama said. She'd boil a chicken in that pot, shred the meat, set aside three-quarters for chicken salad, and the other quarter, plus bones and skin, would go back into the pot of newly created broth. A couple of ladles of broth into a mixing bowl of Red Band flour, and in just a bit, there was a sheet of dough, ready for the trimming with the butcher knife. "Don't roll it too thin, keep 'em thick and it won't get slimy." Mama always made this al dente, an expression we never would have used, calling it "half raw" instead.

• • •

The problem with the good old days is that they don't seem all that good when they are actually taking place. Looking back, I was a complainer in the good old days. It was a time when there was always something to do, and the low man on the totem pole, me, the youngest, got the jobs no one else wanted. This meant silking the corn when everyone else was shucking, or fetching this bucket from the yard, or dragging that one to the field. It meant dumping the enormously heavy pickling crock's awful smelling green juice as close as I could without splashing the grass in the yard. Any spillover would convict me in just a few days, as the mixture was more effective than

Roundup. Sweet pickles were great, but were they worth the trouble? Corn was essential, but how much could we really eat, and what exactly was I supposed to do with a cubic ton of cobs, fleeced of their kernels, and how could I prevent the various critters of the night from inevitably dragging them back into the yard?

We laughed about how, even after everyone had moved out, Daddy never accounted for a smaller household when it came time to plant the garden. The allotment of the farm that had gone to tobacco in the 1970s was just right for corn. A suggestion that a quarter acre each of beans or potatoes might be a bit much, would be answered by, "You like to eat, don't you? You won't complain when you have it in January."

Tomatoes were a serious business, and I finally achieved some level of self-proclaimed prestige the first year they placed me in charge of the crop. This was by default, since no one was around, and coincided with Daddy's decision that we upgrade our technique. This new and improved method required me to drag out the old tobacco sticks, those splinter shrapnel sharing, black widow spider harboring stakes and drive them into the ground between each plant. That was to be followed by using a spool of itchy, skin wrenching twine strung under the bottom leaves of the plants and then adding additional strings as the plants grew. It was labor intensive, annoying and more aggravating to take up when the season ended. However, management had spoken, and labor did not get arbitration.

Admittedly, after all that, picking the tomatoes was easy, and Mama canned enough to make any Italian grandmother proud. This was an essential element for spaghetti, soups, any number of sauces, and sometimes as its own stand-alone dish, garnished with crushed up saltine crackers. My harvest happened in stages. Anything mostly red was picked with the top left in place, that green, odd smelling piece of the stem closely resembling a court jester's collar. The tomatoes went stem down on the picnic table to continue ripening until Mama called for them. The best time of the summer was when the green onions, tomatoes and cucumbers would all be ready at the same time. We filled a bowl that was never big enough with chopped versions of each, floated in apple cider vinegar and dusted with generous shakes of pepper and salt. About twice a month, I'd pick very large green tomatoes to be sliced, dredged in flour, and fried to go with that night's dinner. In season, we did yellow squash or eggplant or yellow onions the same way.

This was everyday fare. Except for hominy and pork and beans, I never remember eating a vegetable from a commercial can until my 20s. It never occurred to me that this was unusual. I remember my disappointment at tasting my first baked sweet potato in a restaurant, when such an item was rare on menus. It was stringy, and I realized why the waiter had brought so much cinnamon, brown sugar and butter — to make it more agreeable. I couldn't figure out how something as perfect as the sweet potato could reach such a condition, especially in this part of the world. Later, a farmer friend told us the supplier had skipped the essential curing stage. After all, there were many occasions when Daddy and his friends sat in the yard with pocketknives and eat sweet potatoes raw, pulled from the smokehouse.

I live with my family on what was a piece of the old farm, but I don't remember exactly when the field shrunk to a garden and then to a box. I suppose it coincided with a diminishing labor force and my parents' decreasing mobility. I worked hard to do my share of planting and weeding and harvesting and storing, but they worked harder. Mama's freezer and shelves now sport grocery store cans of vegetables and there are commercial packs in the freezer. She favors a stir-fry mix now, which is ironic. While we grew loads of peppers and carrots and broccoli, we never once cooked them together in one pan, or had soy sauce on hand. She likes to buy produce in the grocery section, but only the Lord knows where that stuff comes from. Sometimes she's able to source things from local farmers, but so many have had to grow too large and focus on just a couple of crops, that selection just isn't what it used to be. People who think food comes from the grocery store, not someone's dirt, want it easy and fast to prepare, already clean, and most importantly, cheap.

I can't blame them, really, for not thinking about the sweat both from physical labor and mental worry of the farmer. I'm the son of farmers and didn't consider it in my childhood. It was just what we did.

Mama is approaching 90 now and feeble enough that she doesn't leave her easy chair often. Daddy passed away a couple of years ago, bedridden for much of his last half decade and her health declined rapidly. It's hard to imagine her not conducting her kitchen, but that time arrived. Back troubles and hands gnarled from arthritis have kept her from the stove and we can only talk about times past and what we ought to do soon. Why don't we, we always say.

If you look hard enough, you can find good vegetables and meat, but it is not as easy as it used to be, when I only had to walk out to the freezer, or the pantry in the storage building, or the smokehouse and grab what was needed for that night's table. Nostalgia says it all tasted better back then, and I think mostly that it did. Maybe it is because that food touched no hands, in the entire course of its life, that didn't love me. All those days with my hands in the broad diversity of the soil that made up the land where I ate and slept and dreamt of escaping seem so long ago. There was red-orange clay nearest the road, where hardly anything flourished, but it quickly dropped off to darker and richer and deeper ground, the kind that held water and kept roots, nourished them and provided a bounty unmatched.

2
Those Old Barns

"Is there anything you want before I take this thing down?" my friend Brandon asked. He had the heavy late summer sun to his back, cutting a tall figure in his plain white t-shirt and work-worn jeans. "Because you know once I get started..."

"Nah, I can't imagine," I said, shading my eyes, mostly surprised that after lots of talking about it, my folks had found someone to demolish their old tobacco barns. I started to walk over to my house next door, but then stopped and turned around.

"Actually, I do, man," I said. "I want the basketball rim... and the door off that barn there." I pointed to the red tobacco barn that faced my property. I do not know what compelled me in that moment to ask for either item.

Brandon laughed and wiped some sweat from his face with his shirttail. Maybe he was expecting me to ask for a beam or some bricks. "Alright, I'll set them to the side for you. Let me know if you want anything else."

We talked for a minute or two about his primary business, raising hogs, and then he went back to work, pulling off large pieces of old tin and stacking them neatly in piles to transport to his farm at the other end of the county where they'd one day see life again, along with the old rafters and joists of the barns, as a new outbuilding or shop or "man cave."

I'd tried for years to help my mama find someone to help her get rid of the 75-year-plus icons that had become an eyesore. We finally asked

Brandon if he knew someone, and he offered to do the job in exchange for whatever he could salvage. The structures were no longer part of the barnyard, a place that took significant time and sweat and labor from my parents. The barns were interlopers in the yard, a barrier between my lot and my parents' house, once a single farm and now many fractions divided among relatives. Years ago, a widower neighbor had converted one of his old barns into a neat cottage he moved into, yielding the main house to his family, and my parents had floated the idea of renovating the barns and screening in the connecting shelter to make a place for our large family to gather on special occasions. The costs were prohibitive, and now the structures, once essential to the family livelihood, were too far gone.

They weren't much to look at and, in their state of disrepair, they mostly attracted snakes, wasps, weeds and somewhere for the grandkids and great grandkids to get a splinter, get stung, or step on a hiding rusty nail. I was indifferent. Once those barns were down, and grass planted, Mama and Daddy would have one less thing to worry about, and the sprawling mess they'd complained about for years would finally be cleaned up.

Nobody would miss those old tobacco barns.

•   •   •

In the 1950s, it's estimated there were over half a million tobacco barns in North Carolina and today the guess is that fewer than 50,000 are spread over the five tobacco "belts" that tighten around the state: the New Bright, which covers the east; the Border, which butts up against South Carolina; the Old Bright and Middle, which border Virginia and split the Piedmont and Foothills; and the Burley, up in the western mountains touching Tennessee. The barn structures and shapes vary from belt to belt.

In my county that straddles I-95, an hour south of the Virginia border, ours were standard New Bright Belt barns, where tobacco came on strong late in the 19th century. Wooden frame structures about three stories high, they had long, rectangular flues on the roof, and beige concrete, block, and brick foundations with small, square, vented openings in the masonry. Unlike many of our neighbors, our barns were covered in thick, heavy, sheets of lead-like aluminum siding. One was painted red, and the other left silver-gray, although no one remembers why. They were connected by a long pole shelter which covered a workspace that allowed tobacco to be prepared even when a late summer afternoon thunderstorm could pop up at any time and slow the production cycle.

The barnyard was a hive of activity during harvest. Workers brought leaves in from the field, put on a metal conveyor belt called a looper, and stitched with cotton twine to a hardwood stick slightly longer and more stout than a yardstick. The sticks were passed into the barn where workers made a human chain, hanging them on rafters or "tiers" that started five feet from the dirt floor and reached to the very top of the barn. Hanging tobacco was hard, dangerous work.

Daddy cured using burners that looked like mini-kettles and temperatures ran in the mid-100s for days to get the job done. Every farmer had his own way of working the heat to extract moisture from the wet, heavy leaves, converting them from a tarry, sticky, breath-stealing, fume-emitting foul weed to a golden-brown, light, leathery, sweet-smelling final product. The aroma of curing tobacco enveloped not just the county, but most of the state from late summer through mid-September. It was a musky, earthy, scent, and it smelled like money to farmers and buyers alike, as Durham and Winston-Salem and Richmond factories awaited the golden leaf so they could use it to roll profits that trickled slowly down to feed a disparate percentage of the population.

I was still a young boy when my family stopped growing tobacco, having worked in the fields only a couple of times. My jobs mostly consisted of running errands and laying those sticks on the looper in between my sisters' layers of tobacco, just before the machine did its stitch work. Later, when it was time to take out the contents of the barn, a giant cardboard band was set out on a burlap sheet. Stripped leaves were dumped on the pile, and a brother tossed me in to jump around and pack the leaves tight, before the corners of the sheet were brought to the middle, tied off, and loaded on a trailer and a pickup truck. The next morning, the harvest headed to warehouses in Wilson, the biggest tobacco market in the world, where buyers from all the major companies would descend to bid and determine the fortunes of families for the next year.

I can remember one of the last years I rode with my folks to the market. Maybe it was Liberty or Bright Leaf Warehouse — I can't remember — but I can still see the enormity of the space, the row upon row of burlap bundles, and the dust coming up from the floor so thick it was suffocating. I watched intently as the auctioneer moved down the aisle, trailed by buyers, his sing-song chant understood only by his immediate audience, not bystanders, and certainly not an adolescent. After a while, my parents made their way to the cramped business office, which featured a waiting room with a large venetian blind that covered a window to the action on the floor, and an assortment of chairs. Everyone was chain-smoking cigarettes except my parents and it was cramped. They all waited patiently for their checks, while I did not, wiggling and pulling on my mama's hand, noting the posters on the wall, such as the one with two small boys younger than me, dressed in overalls, staring at each other, one asking the other in print, "Been farming long?"

Tobacco farming doesn't resemble those ways at all anymore, and I'm not the least bit nostalgic for the toil it required. Cigarettes were always disgusting to me, they made me cough, and other than a brief dalliance by my oldest brother and a brother-in-law, no one smoked in my family, although it seemed most of our visitors did. My mama considered it a terrible habit, which presented a conflict I often questioned, and was answered by Mama with, "you've got to do something to make a living," and by Daddy with, "you like to eat, don't you?"

Long after we cured the last leaf in the late 1970s, the barns still served as a place of work. We used wood heat, and the shelter offered plenty of space for both green and dry wood, forming walls that rose in the heat of the summer and reluctant fall, only to melt away as I wheel-barrowed load after load to the house all winter long, never quite burning it all, but coming close — a sort of game that I paid no mind to, but which concerned Daddy greatly. Daddy never trusted spring and would often drag me out to the woods way too early on a Saturday morning to cut one more load, just to make sure we didn't run out if there was "one last cold spell."

But no matter how much sawing and splitting took place between those barns, that cured leaf smell always lingered, especially on the hot days when the dust inside the barns stirred and the dust motes formed whitish-gray laser beams through the widening crevasses and cracks and gaps in the walls, and through the flues.

The barns became storage units for farm implements and large tools and vise grips and plows and bicycles and anything that might be fixable and returned to service one day, as well as cans of oil and grease guns and boxes of nails and spark plugs and screws and nuts and washers and bolts. The 1960s Farmall was garaged there with a collection of plows, disks, and bush hogs, and there was still enough room for my brother Bill to work on his car late into the hot, buggy summer nights, while I watched from a stool until Mama called me in for bed. Those barns never gave up tobacco, though, and until the day they came down, I found bits and pieces of dried leaves every summer on the dark, hardpan floor.

Even after Bill converted the area into a welding shop, in the evenings after he and his help went home for supper, there was always the hint of that smell, lingering in the heat, the sound of frogs and crickets offering a background cacophony that remained unchanged even after all the people around it had.

· · ·

"You might want to go ahead and grab your stuff, before it gets accidentally hauled off," Brandon said with a smile one afternoon. He had stripped the barns down to a wooden skeleton, foreign and looming larger, reverse engineered, the exposed timbers still holding strong.

We'd been friends a long while, and now our kids were too, and I was glad to see him salvaging and repurposing the materials. Farms are all about recycling, after all. I envied what I imagined he might build with those rough-skilled hands.

I threw the old basketball goal in the back of Daddy's utility vehicle, and reached for the barn door, not realizing how heavy it was. Having swung it open and closed, and latched it countless times for decades, I'd never considered how substantial it was freed from its support. The weathered 1x4s showed no gap, and were supported by two perpendicular boards on the back, with a third plank serving as a crossbar. Thick, rust-crusted metal plates reinforced what was the interior side of the door, and dozens of dark nails were evenly spaced and bent into the wood on the other side. The hinges, now separated from the doorjamb, seemed twice as large and much heavier than their modern counterparts.

"Need some help?" Brandon asked. Out of pride, I shook my head, and strained to load it.

I rode the short distance to my house, having no idea what to do with my newly acquired pieces, but determined to give them both another life. I tossed the goal under the deck steps, and leaned the barn door against the side of the house, sure I'd figure out something that weekend. Both pieces remained undisturbed for half a decade.

• • •

My best memories of the tobacco barns have nothing to do with work. The barn closest to my parents' house was just the right size to serve as a stand-in batter/backstop for my youthful baseball dreams. The door was made of a spongy, pressboard material. With my brothers grown, and no neighbors my age, the barn was the perfect catcher for my exploits as a Boston Red Sox reliever, saving countless games for John Tudor or Dennis Eckersley. Eventually, one too many fastballs knocked a hole in the door. Daddy was not happy and covered the doorway with corrugated metal. No more World Series were decided.

On the same side of the barn, my older brothers welded a basketball goal with a plywood backboard for me for my birthday one year. It was a rare afternoon from that point that I didn't spin jump shots for at least an hour a day. The hard-packed barnyard soil was perfect, just soft enough to scratch out a three-point line and free throw mark on Friday that would last a full weekend. The barn was the ultimate backstop and my house became the destination of choice for my friends, because the barns meant almost all errant shots and passes would be stopped and deflected. By high school, the games got rougher and more intense, and many a 3-on-3 contest was halted to let tempers cool after a baseline drive ended in a hip check, the crumpling sound of shoulders into that old sturdy siding echoing the foul.

I got a used go-cart for Christmas when I was twelve, and I turned the path around the barnyard into a racetrack. My first set of wheels was red and rusty with a weathered, white vinyl seat, no roll bar and a nimble three horsepower engine. The "Dukes of Hazzard," the hottest show at the time, inspired many slides and spins and donuts, although I never got the courage to jump anything. I slung around, only stopping when I ran out of gas or threw the chain, both of which happened with regularity.

Later on, Bill taught me how to drive a stick shift, going around those barns in his baby blue 1981 Ford Courier, following the two-track laid down by years of pickups and tractors. There was just enough incline to learn clutch-gas tension, and the sharp turns without power steering were good practice for when I saved up for a 1984 Chevette. Almost a decade later, I taught my future wife how to drive a stick so she could fulfill her dream of owning her own pickup truck, a dark green Nissan.

We stood in front of that barn door one afternoon and looked out across a tobacco field-turned cornfield-turned soybean field and envisioned where our future home would be, where we'd plant trees, park vehicles, and chase kids across the yard.

When we finally built that house, the first thing we saw every morning when we left for work was that barn door. Those barns offered great ambush potential during snowball and water gun fights, held curing sweet potatoes, and served as a kitten nursery for strays more than a few times. A shed snakeskin could be counted on several times a year, and I once found an arrowhead after a hard rain, right up under the eaves.

• • •

No one seemed to know an exact date they were built, but the tobacco barns were into their third generation of service when I came along. They survived Hurricanes Hazel, Bertha, Fran and Floyd, when trees and other nearby buildings didn't. The tin rattled and wrenched every storm, but stood strong. In the end, they were no match for my friend and his diligence, and eventually his backhoe and dump truck. It was slightly disorienting the first day I passed where they were supposed to be, but no longer were; replaced by an empty space, and a clear view of my house once I rounded the last curve. In just one season, where grass had never grown, a swath of green flowed from my house to that of my parents, undivided, and now, to newcomers and the youngest members of the family, there is no reason to think it hasn't always been that way. There is a space now, open. It seems small, and unbelievable that two three-story buildings once occupied the void.

One day, years later, I finally brought that door out of the yard, realizing that in my lack of imagination I had neglected the lone remaining artifact from a way of life that has all but disappeared. A moment of inspiration offered a use not long after: the door would become a table. It will be heavy, imperfect, but sturdy and reliable and authentic. I thought about having a woodworker turn legs for it, but then we considered that an old wine barrel from a local secondhand store might be even better. The door is rough and there probably isn't enough sandpaper to change that, but it's okay because that door once did a job and that's part of the appeal.

Bulk barns and mass production farms have no use for the titan flue-curing sentinels of my childhood. Soon, only photographs in books and museums will offer proof they ever existed, gone the way of plow mules and outhouses and country stores, koans that held on way past their primes.

I think about the cold, damp air of the shelter, the pieces of leaves, the chipped paint and peeling siding. Sometimes, I think I still smell that toasted leaf lingering in the crisp fall air, an aroma that defies its final product, but reminds me of another time. I expect when my door is cut and trimmed, it will release that back to me.

3

Homegrown Tomatoes

Only two things money can't buy
That's true love and homegrown tomatoes
–Guy Clark

Apparently, as a tomato farmer, I peaked in my teen years. The summer I was thirteen, I was promoted to Head of Tomato Production on my parents' farm and believed I was at last being recognized for my smarts and responsibility. Tomatoes were a staple on the table and a huge part of the winter inventory in the pantry. My ego would only come into check weeks later on a hot, sweaty morning when I realized not only was I management, I was the entire labor force. Neither position would prove lucrative. All of my brothers and sisters had gotten married, moved out of the house, and were raising small children, so my merits weighed less than the fact that I was the last man standing.

"This year, we are going to do things different," Daddy said as we stood at the edge of the field, the sharp border where the backyard ended. "It's going to be nice and neat. After you get the plants in the ground, you need to put a tobacco stick in between every plant. Then, when the plants start growing, you're going to get the bailing twine and start stringing up under the leaves of the plant, all the way up."

"Hm." I considered protesting, but experience told me there were no labor rights in this organization.

"Go on," Daddy said. "Don't be messing around."

One afternoon a few weeks later, he showed up with his pickup truck loaded with bales of wheat straw for me to tuck under the leaves to keep the just-forming globes from touching the ground and rotting. There would be weeds to chop, manure and other fertilizers to apply, and of course, a liberal dusting of Sevin for the hornworms and stink bugs and aphids.

This project was serious business. In a "garden" that covered acres, the allotment for tomatoes was three dozen plants. My dreams of an air-conditioned summer spent reading James Bond novels and an assortment of Time-Life series ranging from the Civil War to World War II and playing as much ball as possible evaporated into the already wet blanket, gnat-infested late spring/early summer of eastern North Carolina.

I dreaded the work. But all — or most — of the whining I did inside my head and the complaining under my breath went away when Mama used her worn, wooden-handled butcher's knife to slice a Corvette-red tomato the size of softball. Juice dripped all over her calloused hands onto the plate and cream-colored formica counter, as one perfect, thin slice after another mounded. Soon enough, as I took a bite of the first tomato sandwich of the summer, the sweat, my cut up hands, and the bug bites fell away to the best taste of the farm. After all, there is nothing like a homegrown tomato.

•   •   •

The best use of a homegrown tomato is in a sandwich, and the classic tomato sandwich of my youth was a very simple, quick, easy, and satisfying meal, usually lunch. Two super-soft slices of Merita white bread were liberally slathered in Duke's Mayonnaise. Thin slices of dripping red tomatoes, waiting patiently on a plate, having been salt and peppered and dashed with White House apple cider vinegar were piled on as high as the sandwich maker dared. Manners might dictate that a sandwich be eaten on a plate, but often they were consumed over the kitchen sink. A proper tomato sandwich will leak and spill and splatter, and a really good one might require the consumer to change shirts when done, unless there was foresight to tuck a dish towel into the shirt collar.

There were simple rules to sandwich construction. Never toast the bread and use no mayo besides Duke's. There is something about the creamy tanginess of that brand that simply can't be touched, and just about every Southerner swears by it. Variations and experiments on the tomato sandwich were and are allowed, of course. Bacon and lettuce are the king and queen of tomato sandwich royalty.

I've added twists to the tomato sandwich over the years. A drizzle of extra virgin olive oil, or balsamic or rice vinegar can give an exotic feel. Sea salt or Himalayan salt can add some texture. In our current low-carb driven world, substitutes like flax-based Joseph pita bread work just fine, but usually need to be folded over instead of pocketed, because of the saturation of juice and vinegar and oil and Duke's. Regardless, a piece of bread has to be saved to sop up the puddled goodness left in the plate at the end of the meal.

•   •   •

Mayonnaise is a territorial subject, but across the South, Duke's is a dominant player — a brand that is over 100 years old. Until 2006, Duke's came in a glass jar with a yellow label and a black badge proclaiming the name in white script. It's remained basically the same, true to the simple idea of its matriarch and underappreciated inventor.

Eugenia Thomas of Columbus, Georgia, married Thomas Duke in 1900. The couple moved to Greenville, South Carolina shortly afterwards. During World War I, when nearby Camp Sevier National Guard Training Center got busy, Eugenia began selling chicken salad, pimento cheese, and egg salad sandwiches for ten cents each. Her creations were so good that for years after the war, soldiers wrote her for recipes. She opened Duke's Tea Room inside the Ottaday Hotel in Greenville and sold sandwiches in local drugstores.

In 1923, her top salesman convinced Duke that it was her tangy mayonnaise that made her sandwiches special, and that she should shift focus to her homemade dressing. She sold her sandwich business and set up production in an old coach factory. By 1929, Duke could barely keep up with demand for her product and subsequently sold the company to family-owned C. F. Sauer Company in Richmond, giving the brand nationwide distribution. Duke later started Duchess Sandwich Company on the west coast, making her one of the most successful businesswomen of the early twentieth century who started two companies that have survived more than one hundred years.

It's hard to describe what makes Duke's so good. The ingredients are similar to most other brands, but something happens that can't be matched when it is combined with a fresh tomato. Maybe it is best described in their new marketing phrase on the lid — "It's got Twang." It might be because there is no sugar added, unlike many other brands. Perhaps there is a chemical reaction beyond my understanding, but the juice of a bursting ripe tomato drips and mixes and makes the most perfect dressing that sometimes has people licking plates or dipping their fingers into the leavings to get the last taste.

Or so I've heard.

• • •

Despite years of growing tomatoes, something odd happens to the grower when the small fruits first appear. There is a strong desire to pick one before it is ready. It's a combination of anticipation, impatience, and paranoia about bugs or disease or splitting or rotting or something that almost always makes the less disciplined farmer too eager for the first wave of tomatoes. I'm sure this is how fried green tomatoes got their start — someone just couldn't wait, and didn't want to waste the tomatoes, but couldn't eat them. When all else fails in the Southern kitchen, there is one surefire fix. Coat whatever it is in a light dusting of flour and throw it in some hot oil. It works not just for tomatoes, but also for squash, eggplant, zucchini, and okra, among other sometimes-questionable vegetables.

Tomato plants grow quickly, especially when there is plenty of rain. After the initial installation of the old tobacco sticks — a piece of 2x2 wood that was used to hold stitched-on tobacco leaves for curing — my work was just beginning. Every week as the plants climbed and spread, I added another row of twine. Daddy offered regular critiques of my work, often less than tender and sometimes with "dammit" attached. On a day I was particularly inept, "dumbass" might be added. Looking back, it bothered me more then than it does now — memories of those times bring a smile. To be fair, I was overly eager to get done and get on to something else. I'd hear "Tighten up that string," or "Don't let those bottom tomatoes touch the ground" — he could see my faults from edge of the yard all the way down the row, even when the fruits were the same color as the plants. I'd learn much later the value and importance of this advice. When the straw bales arrived, I cut them apart with my pocketknife, and spread bunches both as a protective mulch at the base of the plants, and to keep the low-hanging fruit off the ground and out of rot.

The old bailing twine we had was not like the coated, smooth, plastic stuff of today. It was more like small rope, stringy and rough, and it would work my hands over, dealing out small cuts and rope burn when pulled too tight or twisted.

A lot of work went into those tomatoes on our farm. It seemed also that a lot of money did too, and being a naïve, but all-knowing teenager that summer I wondered why we just didn't buy tomatoes at the grocery store like most everyone else — but at that stage in my life, my experience with store-bought tomatoes was limited to the salad bars at Pizza Inn and Western Sizzlin'. Who knew what they really tasted like, buried under a cascading waterfall of Catalina dressing?

Supermarket tomatoes are known for blandness, and there are a number of reasons for this. Tomatoes that are mass-produced have been hybridized and genetically modified to be resistant to disease, pests, and travel conditions so that there's just not much taste left. Marketing has led to "vine-ripened" designations on shelves, with stems still attached to imply they are fresh off the vine. Almost all grocery store tomatoes are selected to be uniform in size and shape and the outer skin must be perfect.

Many homegrown tomatoes are hybrids as well. We mostly planted hybrids called Better Boys or Beefmasters. The immediacy of harvest offers a freshness that makes them superior, just like most vegetables, when they go from field to table in a matter of minutes.

The very best tomatoes are the heritage varieties or heirloom tomatoes. Those plants that haven't been mixed and matched and remain basically the same as they were one hundred years ago. Heritage varieties are the luxury cars of tomatoes. They are far from uniform, and to be honest, can be ugly as sin, misshapen and imperfect in appearance. Much like people, it is what's on the inside of a tomato that truly sets it apart and makes it special. I've experimented with growing Brandywines and Box Car Willies and Mortgage Lifters — all delicious, but I've yet to find one more tasty or peculiar looking than the Purple Cherokee, the Rolls Royce of heirlooms. The skin is an amalgam of green, red, black, and purple and the fruit often grows wide more than round. The Purple Cherokee is the top-of-the-line, religious experience tomato, full of flavor, a perfect balance of sweetness and acid, soft, little to no hardness or a bitter core, dripping with juice, and not too many seeds, easy on the system to those prone to reflux. The perfect tomato.

•   •   •

Elementary school kids everywhere get excited upon finding out that tomatoes are fruits, not vegetables. This seems contrary considering tomatoes are part of the nightshade family, which includes eggplants and peppers, and unlike fruits, grow in a garden, not on trees in an orchard.

This designation has an interesting and very American backstory. In 1883, the United States placed a tariff on imported vegetables, but not fruits. The Nix family of New York filed a case against the collector of the port at New York, using that fruit designation to help keep the price of tomatoes down.

Tomato plants originated in South America and were brought to Spain with the conquistadors in the 1600s. The plants didn't really catch on in Europe until the nineteenth century, but shortly after the Declaration of Independence, records appear of tomato growing by the colonists. Thomas Jefferson recorded growing tomatoes in 1781. Maybe if I'd known that as a teenager it would have helped inspire me. It should have been in those biographies I was itching to get back to, literally and figuratively, as I bent over plants, wiping sweat and swatting insects.

• • •

There is a lot involved in growing tomatoes. Secrets are made and kept regarding planting times, fertilizer, pest control, times of day to water. One summer, Daddy and his best friend got into a tomato controversy. Although I can't recall the details, other than one accused the other of cheating or sabotage, whatever that could mean. They went about a month without speaking and never seemed to get completely over it.

Planting and stringing the tomatoes was just the beginning. In eastern North Carolina, there is much soil quality variation, not just from farm to farm, but even on the same plot of land. In my younger years, we planted much of our small acreage with tobacco and later hay and soybeans. One plot, on the backside of my parents' simple home was set aside for the garden, which heavily featured corn, sweet potatoes, string beans (we called them "snaps"), and butter beans, in addition to the tomatoes. The soil nearest the road was hard and heavily weighted with orange clay, but within just a few rows, it changed over to rich ash-to-black loamy soil. Every spring, when it was turned over for the first time, the dirt felt soft and lush as I pulled up double handfuls and let it sift through my hands onto my bare feet. There was a moistness and fine grain to it, something special, a distinct aroma that even to this day I have a hard time putting to words — at once clean and musky and pleasing to the senses. Usually, all sorts of flying insects hovered just above the soil, dancing in their own celebration of spring. The ground smelled like it was ready to grow something.

In those days, I never lingered for long, sometimes taking a few minutes to build a frog house or two by packing dirt around my pushed-together feet and then carefully removing them.

After the tomatoes were in the ground, I'd drag several linked-together water hoses attached to the backdoor spigot to the edge of the field. Daddy neatly furrowed the rows after several passes on the rusting red 1960s Farmall, ending at a small two-track before the neighbors' fenced-in cow pasture. That was the job I coveted, but later, when I finally got my chance, I realized that I'd underestimated the old man's precision and skill. Nice, pushed up hills were ready for plants, and allowed water to run down the gently sloping rows. I typically watered right after supper until the edge of dark, just enough time for the well's current to reach the end of the row. We skipped watering only on days when thunderstorms offered relief, and the plants grew tall and lush and deep green. They produced yellow flowers, each representing a future delicious tomato, and attracting pollinating bees, which were essential, but were a hazard at harvest. The plants embraced the oppressive heat that I spent much effort to avoid.

Tomatoes offer a pungent fragrance that stays with you upon touch, much like basil — a mix of rain, fresh flowers, and tart fruit, pleasing and foretelling of the goodness to come.

I was up early each morning to pick. In the first few days, I could usually fit the day's haul in an old red, metal egg basket, but soon, I had to lug woven cane bushel baskets with thin metal handles down the row. The baskets were sturdy, but the heavy gauge wire cut into my hands as the basket filled with dense, heavy fruits.

Picking tomatoes is not as simple as it sounds. Once they were mostly red, it was time to come off the vine. Waiting a day could be ruinous because of bugs, rot, or splitting. It was important to pick and leave the stem in place. This is where tomato-ists deviate about when the time is right to pick. Many people let the tomato fully ripen to a deep red on the vine. Ours were often so large they broke the plants if we left them on too long, so I picked them when they were "mostly" red and hauled them to the two picnic tables in the backyard. The tables stood in the shade one of the large, ancient pecan trees. I carefully sorted by ripeness, stem down to allow them to finish ripening.

Critics will say that tomatoes will rot if left to ripen this way. Others suggest putting tomatoes in a brown paper bag to let them finish. All of this may be true, but the sheer volume dictated my strategy, and relatively few were lost. By the height of the season, I had two picnic tables and all four benches covered in tomatoes, all in various stages of ripening.

My sisters would come from their homes to help Mama, and they spent days at the time canning tomatoes in quart jars, peeling and boiling an enormous inventory that would end up as spaghetti sauce or soup or base for Sunday beef roasts. The work didn't stop until each of them had enough for their families for the year. Most every night of the summer, we ate sliced tomatoes soaked in vinegar and dusted with salt and pepper, served as a side dish, or combined with cucumbers and fresh green onions, all from the garden. Sometimes, the tomatoes were stewed, dished into bowls and topped with crushed saltines.

Mama's soup was the best, probably because it had everything imaginable included. Ground beef, stringed chicken, pasta, every vegetable we grew, all floating in a rich, tangy tomato base. Salt, pepper, and sugar were added to tame the acidity, and sometimes a bay leaf. It was best for a winter lunch, but always a treat. During the high traffic days of Mama's kitchen, no matter the time of day, I never saw anyone ever turn down a bowl. They usually asked for seconds.

• • •

I spent so much time in the field growing up, I swore I'd escape the hardship one day. When I became an adult, I would use farmer's markets and stores. I wouldn't be old-fashioned, growing tomatoes in a garden. That didn't last long. It wasn't just about taste, though, it was more than that. A call to work the land, to stay true to tradition, pulls hard and that life I wanted to get away from wouldn't let me go. There is a pride that comes from growing one's own food — 250 years of turning the North Carolina soil in my family's past had set roots.

My recent efforts at growing tomatoes have not gone well. After getting married and moving out to my own place on the farm, given to us as a wedding present by my parents, my success was mixed. This was in the 1990s, and I had less time and there seemed to be more work involved. I planted a row in the ground next to the house with peppers and tomatoes, but my yields were a joke compared to my parents. I tried for years, on and off. Even with poor results, I couldn't resist. I tried raised beds, sure I'd get great results in a smaller, controlled space. Bugs, disease, rotting, splitting, and defects showed otherwise. I tried container growing. I changed plant varieties. I used newspaper shreds as mulch, in place of hay.

Is the memory of my successes a generation back real or imagined? I wonder if I have idealized the time and the results. It is a fact that I picked hundreds of tomatoes, if not more, and everyone could see the Mason jars that filled the pantry. Remembrances have emerged and I recall throwing many, many rotten tomatoes into the pasture, much to the pleasure of the grazing cows. The results were real, and I now realize that the oversight of my parents, their knowledge and wisdom, which I was sure as a teenager I didn't need, was the difference. Their love and guidance, and their corrections held me to a standard that I wouldn't have set for myself.

Hope and optimism continue to abound regarding my crop each year. Following a discouraging past season where I attempted only four plants, volunteers from those Purple Cherokees appeared, nearly a dozen. The previous year's disappointment literally became the next year's potential. We've used containers and old newspapers and coffee grounds and a mix of the farm and "store bought dirt" to compensate for our mostly clay-side of the old farm. When the heart of summer approaches, there are dozens of tomatoes of various sizes hanging from our plants, but never the same output as the days of my youth.

Recently, I brought my two young sons into the effort. The legacy of growing and producing food, and farming, built over two centuries, is more fragile than I ever considered as a teenager. It can disappear in a single generation, as has been proven. Like so many things, what I thought would remain forever has passed. And yet, things look promising. We won't can or freeze any tomatoes, but hopefully soon, we will be flush in sandwiches, soups, and homemade salsa.

A longtime family friend has a tomato business nearby, just outside the county seat of Nashville. He grows his crop in water, a process called hydroponics, an idea that would have garnered gap-mouthed wonder in my childhood. The tomatoes are delicious, far better than anything available in a store. They are a great stop-gap, but even in their goodness, they can't top a homegrown tomato in my dirt-stained hand, or in my mind.

4
Homeplace

The snake appeared out of nowhere. It came right at me, moving and sliding across the dirt and grass in that lilting, cursive S shape. I was about four years old, playing in the shade of my daddy's old pickup, trying to make frog houses and highways for my hand-me-down Matchbox cars. The snake was casting its tongue and hissing and coming to get me. I pushed myself up out of the dirt and started yelling.

Down the rows of tobacco seedlings, there was no one, just waves of heat rising in the distance. My parents and brothers and sisters and the people who alongside them were pegging tobacco had gone over the crest of horizon into the sloping fields that seemed so huge to me then. I'd been left at the end of the row, by the two-track path. I tried to get myself off the ground to run, but panic set in.

I wasn't a fast runner and never would be. I took off, screaming, certain I was going to die, the fear of snakes having been ingrained in me from the cradle. This snake was long and dark and scaly and I surely knew was out to bite me and poison me and kill me. No matter where I moved, it followed.

"Help me! There's a snake tryin' to bite me! Help! Help!"

Suddenly, a man appeared, tall and lanky. Dust lingered in the air where he had come running down the rows wide open, those long legs closing ground. He had a hoe in his hand and in one instant went from the field to between me and the monster serpent.

"I got it, Michael," the man said, calm, but out of breath. "Don't worry 'bout it."

He swung the hoe like an ax and with angry force. He short-armed the hoe again, and the snake's head detached from its body. It still looked like it was hissing. I got behind the man and grabbed the back of his leg, not ready to believe I was safe yet. By this point, my mama and brothers and sisters had appeared—what had taken them so long?

"He ain't gonna hurt you, now," the man laughed. Then he did something crazy. He reached down and grabbed the snake's body, which was unwinding from its S, still twitching and writhing, searching for its head. He took a couple of steps, cocked his arm back, and threw the snake into a tree in the old cemetery next to the field. It did not come down.

I stood looking up with my mouth open. "You saved my life."

The man picked up the hoe, grinning as he headed back to work down the row. "It won't nothing. I got you, little man. You holler if you see another one."

By this point, Mama had picked me up and was sitting on the tailgate, checking on her baby, worried, apologizing for not checking on me sooner, quarreling that nobody had kept an eye on me even though they were supposed to. Between her assurances and scolding, I kept on and on about how that snake was going to bite me and kill me and how the man had gotten there just in time. But I had a question.

"Why did he throw that snake in a tree?"

"Because Martin is crazy," Mama said. She didn't add further embellishment.

Some said that if you kill a snake and throw it in a tree, it will rain. It had not rained for days. I remember because the farmers around us had complained and fretted about rain constantly. Only heat and dust and misery. Others said that was a bunch of superstitious shit.

It rained that night, a hard thunderstorm with lightning. As I lay in bed, I wondered if the snake had washed out of the tree.

And so my first memories of the Homeplace were of fear and danger.

• • •

The Homeplace was where my daddy's daddy had grown up. A few previous generations lived there and raised crops, drawing life from the land.

The old farm was located a few miles away from where we lived, right off of North Carolina Highway 97, a relatively straight road out of Zebulon that runs to Rocky Mount and other points east as it knifes through the rural and sprawling coastal plain. In the days before the bypass, Highway 97 was the way folks in our part of the state got to Raleigh.

Access to the farm made it seem to belong in another world. After turning onto a long winding dirt path, which often became nearly impassable after a hard summer gully washer, the two-track wound its way past surrounding land mostly owned by the Bissettes—a meander much like the path of that snake. Once past the fields, there was a brief, dark border of thick mangy woods. Thorns and kudzu and a swampy creek made it forbidden and impractical to explore. It was a gateway to the past.

About three-quarters of a mile in, there was one last sharp turn, past a sometimes abandoned, sometimes occupied sharecropper's house—it was often difficult to tell one status from the other in the abject poverty of that time and place in the 1970s. When it was occupied, the residents stared when we rode by, not waving, but casting a warning to drive on. Daddy always waved anyway.

Around that last curve, there it was: the old house. The path led to what had been the yard, but was now weeds and dirt, with a magnolia tree for shade. The house seemed like something out of a Depression-era photograph. By then it had been abandoned for at least thirty years, maybe more.

It was a one-story stick house on a squat brick foundation. The windows were mostly lost to vandals—teenagers and vagrants who discovered the house as a place to drink and leave their Pabst and Budweiser cans and a target for the rocks they threw at the old glass windows. It was a spooky place to a young boy, deserted like those haunted houses in the Saturday afternoon movies I watched. At the time of the snake story, my grandfather owned the house and the property, but my parents farmed part and my uncle the other. What little I recall of my grandfather, I suspect there was rent and that it was not let below market price.

•   •   •

It never occurred to me when I was growing up that the abandoned house was probably comfortable in its day. Mama warned us not to play in it, although my brothers and sisters—all at least ten years older than me—usually tested this edict as far as their good sense would allow, taking breaks in the shade and breeze that passed through empty doorways. There had never been electricity or running water or a toilet. Even though some of our neighbors, even into the 1980s, still had outhouses, the thought of using one was outside of my understanding. I never managed more than a peek inside.

There was a cemetery nearby, with names on stones I'd never heard mentioned in my house. The buried were strangers to me, long gone and forgotten. The cemetery was walled but hadn't been well maintained. For a people who put so much value on family, Southerners don't always do a good job tending graveyards. Many have been lost to neglect and vandalism, as well as lack of resources, no trespassing signs, and time. Looking back, I have to think the cemetery was once a peaceful final resting place, shaded with ancient pecan and walnut trees.

And yet, this place meant absolutely nothing to me as a child. I had no connection to the land or the people. I only knew that time spent there—usually announced the day before—meant time away from TV and my toys and books. It was a place of work and bugs and sweat and snakes. It was a place of dangerous things, dangerous creatures, and I suspected dangerous people as well.

•   •   •

That early summer day of the snake attack when my family went to the fields, I was the perfect age to be a nuisance. The job at hand was pegging, sometimes called transplanting, tobacco, which entailed walking the fields looking for dead or dying plants, plucking and replacing them with stronger seedlings. This was done with a wooden peg that was about seven or eight inches long, cylindrically shaped with a broad, rounded tip at one end, and angled and flat at the other end. This allowed a small hole to be dug, usually with a twist of the peg.

Looking back, some of the fine details are sketchy, but the encounter with the snake was not.

The man who saved me was really not a man, at least technically. He was Martin, a teenager from down the road, a family friend who often was among the collection of paid local workers—a diverse group of white and black and young and old, male and female, who shared the trait of having little money. They weren't scared of hard work and few had their own transportation. On these field days, Daddy would be up and out by the time it got light, pulling into yards and blowing horns. He didn't have to worry about waking anybody up—they were eager to go before the heat went from stifling to unbearable, although they worked in both without distinction. Their screen doors slammed shut behind them as they jumped off their porches and into the back of the truck.

While that day it surely seemed the snake was chasing me, it was not likely so. I was certain I'd be bitten and die a painful death, much like the careless settlers who were ambushed by rattlesnakes on TV westerns, but I wasn't in any real danger. Reflecting on everyone's reaction seems to validate that theory. I think that snake might have been a black garden snake—one trying to escape in my general direction. Snakes have been objects of superstition and fear for centuries, perhaps more highly regarded today for their role in the ecosystem, but we did not tolerate them on our land when I was growing up. We certainly lived by the credo that the only good snake was a dead one.

The drama of the situation was real. I'd seen too many Sunday night episodes of *Wild Kingdom* to misunderstand the dangers of nature. Martin was my hero for years after that, and I often brought up the fact that he'd once saved my life, even as the story aged and became silly into my teens. He still lives down the road from me, but I haven't seen him in years.

It is an early memory, the snake attack. If I could paint or draw with any skill, I could transfer that image, me trying to run, the hoe coming down, the blood, the snake's lifeless body twisting through the air like a crooked tree branch. I still remember the way the air smelled—wet and metallic—in the moments before that long-desired thunderstorm brought down its wrath, the way I shuddered when the lightning creased across my bedroom window that night, and the sound of the rain crackling on the old shingles of our house.

•   •   •

When my grandfather died, he left little money, but he had some farmland that was divided between my daddy and my uncle. By that point, Daddy had gotten a public job with a welding company, using the one good thing—clerical skills—he brought home from his army stint in the Korean War, though that wasn't enough to counter the nightmares that also made the return trip. He still farmed a little, rented the Homeplace, and raised some hogs with my brother.

We were not immune to the farm crisis of the late 70s-early 80s, the one that spawned Farm Aid and other calls for awareness, but that charity didn't reach eastern North Carolina in any way I saw. My parents ended up selling the farm to Mr. Bissette who had rented it for years and owned most of the surrounding property. He was their friend and was fine with my daddy riding over anytime he liked without having to call first.

I didn't think much about the sale, other than the sadness it cast on my parents. Sometimes in the summer, after supper, when tobacco and other crops had been in the ground long enough to make a showing, Daddy, Mama, and I would ride over to the Homeplace in the pickup. We'd bounce over the path, sometimes a washboard, other times a muddy mess, to look around. A migrant camp had been constructed just past the old sharecropper house. The people in those concrete block buildings redefined the meaning of poor, a word I'd heard attached to us. No, no, that was not true. Maybe we didn't have much money, but we weren't poor. I stared through the windshield at the dirty, inquiring faces, the children who played in mud holes and with rocks instead of toys, the exhausted, distant looks on the faces of the adults. There seemed to be little hope in that place. As always Daddy waved. They usually waved back.

. . .

After the camp was built, I don't think we rode back over to the Homeplace more than once or twice again.

. . .

Homeplace was a common term I heard growing up. It seemed like almost everyone we came into contact with, whether at the seed store, or grocery store, or church, or anywhere else had something they referred to as the *homeplace*. I'd often hear of people who had left home and then upon the death of a grandparent or parent moved back to the old homeplace.

I hardly ever hear the term anymore and I suppose that's a product of how we've moved farther away from the farm and the agrarian lifestyle in North Carolina and so many other places as well. Farms aren't passed from generation to generation any longer, shrinking as they are broken into shares for descendants. As the small farms give way to the giant farm operations, many are leveled for shopping centers or housing developments with names like Farm-something or something-Acres.

. . .

Dean Webb and Mitchell Jayne of the Dillards (they played the Darlings on *The Andy Griffith Show*) wrote a song that became a bluegrass standard called "The Old Home Place." While it has a light, fast pace, it's a pretty dark tune: a former farm boy bemoans leaving his family's old home for the bright lights and a "girl from the town." He ends up losing his money and the girl, and the house is eventually torn down before he returns. The farm boy regrets it all and wishes he was dead by the time the song ends.

Although for a time my wife and I "hobby" farmed with goats and chickens, I never entertained a thought for one minute that I might make my living from the land. Mama certainly had no intention of me being a farmer. My siblings liked to remind me that, as the youngest, I had it much easier than they did regarding farm life. They were certainly right even though it irritated me when they said it. I was young when my folks abandoned tobacco and livestock as a vocation, but it remained a part-time endeavor until I left home and so I'd say I didn't have it so easy by today's standard.

When I made my last visit to the Homeplace, probably 25 years ago, the fields that in my childhood seemed as vast and rolling as the open prairie were more modest. The house, still eerie, was much smaller, the shade trees shorter. The cemetery was covered in overgrowth, never well-cared for in my grandfather's time, and certainly not valued by owners with no connection. I heard the house was torn down years ago.

It takes time to create value in a place. In the South at least, it seems people have to get some age on them to consider ancestry and genealogy and where they came from. As the future becomes less abstract and certainly not as long and broad, one inevitably starts to consider his identity, and place certainly has a large role.

Now, I'd like to go back and look around that house and imagine waking up each day without a neighbor in sight, no humans but my immediate kin. To work long and hard to make sure there is food to eat. I want to roam the cemetery and read those old stones and see the plot where the bones lie of those names I've now memorized from my past. To be among the ghosts who have the same DNA. What did they think and do and love? Did they read and play music or make corn liquor? Were they teetotalers like my parents? Did they go to church? With a half-century behind me now, I'm saying I'd try to connect.

I'd like to stand at the edge of those fields and wonder what was. I wouldn't even think about that snake at all.

5
Shopping List, 1937

*Rat poison. Cod liver oil. Thyroid tablets. Oil cloth, 1 2/3 yd. red paper &
string. Coffee and coco. Steel wool. Wax paper & napkins.*

In distinct, neat feminine handwriting was the beginning of a shopping list
my Grandma Ruth made on the inside back cover of her checkbook in the
fall of 1937. Over 40 years later, that checkbook was sitting on a desk in her
bedroom, folded, propped open, and ready to be used.

Even though I had little emotional connection to my grandparents, I
couldn't bring myself to throw this and other items in the trash during my
assignment to clear their desk after my grandfather's death, about a year after
my grandmother passed. The budding historian in me was already showing
an inheritance of appreciation for artifacts. I gently placed the checkbook in
a box, took it home with several other items, and put them away for another
40 years.

• • •

On a cold, bright, fall day, we drove out to the old house. I remember us all
wearing heavy coats, and the odd shape of the light as it crept through the
paper-thin glass windows. It was that old glass that gives a swirly effect
looking in and out, an imperfection so different from today's energy
efficient, character deficient sameness. The house was old and dusty and

dirty and smelled strange, this place where my grandparents lived for most of the 20th century. It was drafty and intimidating and ripe to be haunted, I thought. A haze of stale food, pipe smoke, bug spray, and something odd I'd later realize was marijuana, lingered.

My granddaddy — my daddy's daddy — had died about a month before, and the contents of the house had to be dealt with. Daddy had been named executor, so the task fell mostly on him. It was surprising, because even at nine years old, it was clear to me my grandparents favored his older brother — and if it hadn't been, overheard comments made it so.

Thanksgiving was approaching and Daddy and Mama and Daddy's brother Billy wanted to get this done before Christmas. They faced an intimidating task. Part of the two-story, white house was put together with pegs instead of nails and was at once grand and plain and unkempt. It was the home Daddy grew up in, and even though I haven't set foot in it in nearly four decades, the memories remain vivid. There was a dark, wood-paneled sitting room on the backside of the house that included a sweeping staircase that opened to the front foyer. The upstairs included several large rooms that were locked up with all the furniture covered in bed sheets, as if they were in storage. The walls were plaster. The one room occupied by the sketchy caretaker was trashed. The floor was in total contrast to the lower level, open, airy, like something out of a magazine featuring Southern mansions. Dust motes twisted into long bars on the upstairs landing, and in the winter, most windows on the north side offered a view of the Tar River, several hundred yards away, as well as the slum-like, drug infested trailer park my Granddaddy Troy had thought was a good idea for additional income.

Downstairs, where my grandparents spent most of their time, was like a throwback episode of "Hoarders." The kitchen air hung heavy, thick with a closed-up odor, and there were bugs everywhere. One room over, the century-old dining table lay hidden under mounds of bills, trash, half-eaten food, Raid, and knick-knacks. I specifically remember the 1970s red bird with a yellow top hat on an axle that rocked back-and-forth dipping its beak into a glass of water. A small sitting area/living room featured an old Siegler oil heater, and a failing apart couch propped up with bricks and a couple of ripped chairs, the innards sagging and hanging free. Daddy lit the heater to cut the chill and allow work to begin.

Many trips to the county dump were made over the ensuing weeks, as my older brothers and sisters and Mama and Daddy hauled out trash and broken or worn out remains from a life where it seemed the old couple had bought nothing new since Eisenhower left office.

• • •

Cards. Matches. Peanut butter. 2 coconuts. Rice.

My grandparents loved rice pudding and fresh coconut for German chocolate cake, Ruth's favorite. Troy used a work hammer to bang away at the hard brown shells. The never bought the bagged stuff.

• • •

On the other side of the sitting room was the master bedroom. Everyone waded in with trash bags. As I look back now, the adults had the most unpleasant and physically demanding tasks. I was told to clean off the old battered desk that was piled high with papers, pens, pencils, trash, and newspapers, all sorts of detritus of a long life.

People will often say, "It looks like they just left it and never came back," when touring exhibits in museums. My grandparents' home was like a museum, but the lived-in kind. Life happens until it stops and the remainders are left for someone else to deal with. Those things that retained such importance for one person often have no importance to others, the ones tasked with clean up.

With dread, I started and soon became a self-styled Br'er Rabbit. Treasures abounded for a kid who spent an inordinate amount of time studying the old World Book Encyclopedias in our living room at home, poring over American history. On the floor next to the desk were copies of the Raleigh *News & Observer*, most of them dating back to World War II. Some were from the Korean War era, when Daddy served. They were mixed in with more recent issues, as if waiting to be read for the first time, even though it was 1979.

And then, there it was, on the backside of the desk, partially open: an old checkbook. The way it was arranged, it looked as if a check had just been written from it, but closer examination showed the dateline as 193__, and the most recent stub was from the spring of 1938, the oldest from the fall of 1937. Before I was done, I'd retrieved the family's 1943 ration books, an old pocket watch, and a fountain pen, among other papers. I ran off to find Mama, and to find out how much of this cool stuff they'd let me keep.

• • •

Teeny's socks & Billy & Gerald. L.G. plate. Emmogene book. Lee box dishes. Stationary [sic]. *Socks. Underwear 40.*

This was Ruth's shopping and Christmas list. "Teeny" was Daddy's nickname. While a big man of six feet and well over 200 pounds as an adult, he was undersized as a baby, with dark curls so charming, he won a Sears Roebuck Baby Contest in 1933. There is a small portrait and engraved silver cup in my parents' house that commemorates it. Billy was his older brother, and Gerald was a cousin I don't remember. L.G. was Lester Gold Brantley, my great-uncle, a kind man and voracious reader I used to wish was my granddaddy. Or, it might have been his warm, educated son, a junior who went by "Gold," and was born in 1937. He went on to be a teacher, and when he passed, his brother gave me Gold's extensive book collection. I don't know who Lee was. Socks must have been in short supply. I assume the underwear was for Troy, he was probably a size 40 in those days. It's hard to say, as there are very few photographs of my grandparents prior to "old age."

• • •

1937 was a big year. War clouds were darkening in Europe. Japan invaded China and sunk the USS Panay near Nanking, claiming not to have seen the American flags painted on the deck. The incident turned American opinion against the Japanese and foreshadowed Pearl Harbor. Amelia Earhart disappeared, the Hindenburg crashed, and FDR was trying to extract the United States from the Great Depression and threatening to expand and pack the Supreme Court. Spam was invented; the sort-of meat thing, not the bulk email. The first issue of *LOOK* magazine hit the streets and DC Comics was birthed. Daffy Duck, Morgan Freeman and Waylon Jennings were born. King Edward married Wallis Simpson. The Golden Gate Bridge opened. "Snow White" was in theaters, Steinbeck's *Of Mice and Men* and Hurston's *Their Eyes Were Watching God* came off the presses, and Tolkien gave the world *The Hobbit*.

Things were quieter in sleepy North Carolina. Democrat Clyde Hoey was governor. He made his name by appointing a black man to the board of trustees of a black college. Hoey was against integration, but for segregated higher education for blacks — he also publicly stated he was against civil rights. He opposed a third term for FDR, even though they were in the same party. Later, as a U.S. Senator, he opposed statehood for Hawaii. The tobacco and cotton farm support programs that lasted until the next century started. My grandparents on both sides, and my parents, benefitted from these programs, the last in a multi-century line of farmers.

In Nash County, where my grandparents lived, things weren't much different than they had been in the previous century. The big news was that the Rural Electrification Administration was sending $16 million for electric lines to the area. Electricity was promoted by informing citizens that the average monthly bill in the county was $3.23. Ads dominated newspapers for "good young mules" and many dealers offered to take trade-ins.

Besides farming, my grandparents briefly ran a country store after Daddy got back from Korea. Ruth, an old maid for years, had income from land she had accumulated through purchase and inheritance across two counties. One parcel she owned now contains a prison. The average house cost $4,100 and the average annual salary was $1,780 a year. A car could be had for $760 and gas was 10 cents a gallon, a loaf of bread was a penny less. Phone numbers were often just two digits.

•   •   •

I feel sure anyone else would have bagged and trashed my findings, only because the rest of my family is far more practical and neat than I am, and far less obsessed with history. We didn't have a lot of books — the Bible and mostly the encyclopedias from the mid-1960s, and the yearbook updates they issued each year.

My stash had to be culled. Papers riddled with silverfish and other pests were disposed of, and I could fit what I kept into a leftover third grade folder. After carefully looking through the items, I tucked them away, a newspaper or two, the ration books, and the checkbook. Once cleared, the desk looked as though it might collapse, but Mama saw something else — potential. She took it down the road to a retired man who spent his days resurrecting items that looked like landfill-bound trash into priceless heirlooms and antiques. She repeated this with countless pieces in the same condition, the few things Daddy got from the will, most of the land and the house going to his oldest brother. I used the desk for years to do homework and today it still looks amazing. That's where the folder stayed until just a few years ago.

•   •   •

I was not, as I saw then and know now, missing my grandparents and I was not alone. No one seemed emotional except Daddy. My grandparents were an irascible, bitter, grouchy couple. While it has been over 40 years since their passing, they are rarely mentioned by family, or recalled by friends. Are they forgotten or repressed? It stands out to me because my maternal grandmother, known by Granny Lucy even to those she wasn't related, comes up often, usually with a warm smile and funny recollection of her quirkiness and resiliency.

My grandparents offer few pleasant memories, mostly limited to Ruth laughing at me. Troy usually wore a dress shirt and slacks with a fedora out in public, no matter the occasion, and at his house, usually sat around in a sleeveless, ribbed white undershirt, those dress slacks and no socks. This was particularly unsettling as he lost toes to diabetes and often called attention to it. Typically, he pointed out that someone should spank me more, usually when my inevitable boredom during visits resulted in me wriggling around in a dining room chair with a broken cane bottom that scratched my legs. When I got older, I usually played outside or went to visit the kindly, elderly lady who rented a house on the farm just across the dirt and gravel driveway. There was a point where I felt guilty about my feelings towards Ruth and Troy, but that passed as the reality set in that they simply were not nice people. It happens, but now I'm at the age where it makes me sad, and a little, tiny part of me fears and hopes I'm not passed that recalcitrant inheritance.

• • •

Cups & saucers. Corn flakes. Bes. tonal. Shampoo tint. Light ash blond. 6 5/7.

The most fascinating thing to me about Ruth was always her age. As a child, I marked time with its connection to events in history. Ruth was born in 1891 and I can remember asking her if she remembered the Spanish-American War. She usually just laughed and clapped her hands together. Very many of her male neighbors were Confederate veterans when she was younger. Her grandparents were German immigrants — I never wondered then like I do now what she thought about her relatives in the Old World potentially fighting those in the New World. She was nearly 30 when World War I broke out and married Troy the year Charles Lindberg crossed the Atlantic. He was 10 years her junior.

My daddy was born the year Hitler came to power, when Ruth was 42. He was 36 when I was born, and it always seemed significant to me that while my friends had daddies that were Vietnam veterans, my dad served during the largely forgotten Korean War. I've kept the older parent tradition going, being 31 to 38 when my children were born. I wish I had access to the stories my grandparents could have told me, the history they could have brought to life. But would they? Would I have something to remember them by other than Ruth always wore dresses and horn-rimmed glasses and stockings, no matter the time of day?

That Troy put garden poison on his curing hams to keep out the bugs in the smokehouse? That even as doctors pleaded with him to mind his diabetes (and the fact that he was constantly losing toes), his stubbornness prevailed? What could Troy have told me about my ancestors, who lived and farmed in eastern North Carolina since the 17ᵗʰ century? Shouldn't there be something better to remember?

•   •   •

The remaining checks in the old book resemble today's version in shape and layout, but not much else. There is no digitized string of routing and account numbers. There is not even a pre-printed name or number. These checks had an engraving of a tobacco plant and the name The Planters National Bank and Trust Company, one of the largest banks in North Carolina at the time, and one that eventually through mergers became part of what is now PNC Bank.

The stubbed entries offer a peak into routines that are so different from today. Few checks were written in my grandparent's time, as most transactions were cash. It was understandable following the banking collapse that people were still distrustful of banks. This was the depth of the Depression. Today, we make more swipes in a day and drive farther to work than they did in a month. Then, there was little need or time to leave the farm. There is no organization to the list — they produced all the basics on the farm, from meat to vegetables. Webb's Mill, where corn and wheat could be ground, was within walking distance, just across Highway 64 in a right turn of the Tar River.

On October 9, 1937, Ruth was in Rocky Mount and bought a new pair of leg braces for my Uncle Henry, who had cerebral palsy, paying Dr. Wheeldon $94, which is a little over $1,600 today. She went downtown and wrote another check at Sears Roebuck for $4.82 ($84.21 today) for "merchandise." I assume Troy was with her, as she never drove or had a license.

There are no other entries until preparations for Christmas and end-of-year bills were taken care of. On December 13, 1937, she paid Oettinger's $15 for a permanent. This would be a $262 hairdo today. This is perhaps the most staggering finding for me, as my grandparents were known in polite circles as "frugal," but in hard whispers as "stingy" or "tightwads." I never saw them as generous, and don't recall any gifts at Christmas or my birthday. Surely there must have been some, right?

With so few transactions, and the account being at a Rocky Mount bank, I've concluded that the checkbook was a separate household account. Ruth was from Edgecombe County, next door to Nash and where Rocky Mount straddles the county line. Most of their banking was likely done in nearby tiny Spring Hope. The last three transactions closed out 1937 and ended in the spring of 1938, with no explanation. They made a farm and home insurance payment for $39.34 to B.R. Bissette on the last day of 1937. A trip was made to Sears Roebuck on April 14, 1938, where $3.58 was spent on "mdse." and another $26.44 was cut to Mutual Life Insurance Companies for their policies. I don't know if the account was closed, or new checks issued, or why the checkbook was kept around almost a half century after its last use.

And now I realize that my relationship has matured with my grandparents all these years later. I didn't enjoy visiting them; they didn't dote on their youngest grandson. But now, with insight into their day-to-day lives, and with several years as a parent under my belt, I see them not warmer, but perhaps more real, people who needed socks and medicine and who liked sweets made with coconut, and vain enough to splurge on expensive salons. They lived in turbulent times, times that wore on them and certainly influenced their behavior. It's sad in a way that they are far more interesting to me in the context of the range of history they experienced than they were alive as my closely connected relatives. Most of my friends have warm memories of their grandparents.

That home I was intimidated by and dreaded going in, prompts me to want to go back and walk through one more time with my historian wife. I think it should be restored and wonder if I should be the person to approach my uncle about it, although it doesn't seem practical and my requests to visit have been declined. It could be grand and wonderful, where it once wasn't, and construct a bridge and a relationship long after its time has passed.

6
Farm to Table Before it was Cool

It was a hot July morning, but then again they were all hot mornings in July. My older sister Jane had spared me the field work, asking me to stay across the road at her house until her babies woke up. I was about 13 and probably wouldn't have kept up or pulled the right ears that went into the back of the tobacco truck pulled by my daddy on his Farmall tractor. My nephews woke up and now it was time for me to bring them over and do my part.

The red antique sputtered into the backyard, under the canopy of the two ancient pecan trees that provided shade in the summer, a shield during dirt clod fights with my cousins, and nuts for eating in the fall and winter. On that day and for several days after, it was the staging area for hundreds of ears of sweet yellow corn. The ears were dumped on a burlap tobacco sheet, a holdover from the farming days, but still with plenty of life purpose left in it.

"I like corn, but not this much," I moaned to my sister. "I don't know if it's worth it."

"I know, but there's nothing like fresh corn," she said. And she was right. I'd never eaten corn out of a can or a frozen bag and wasn't sure who bought those things in the grocery store. Why didn't everyone have a garden? Because it was hard work.

"You ready to shuck some corn," my little mama said, offering an arm swing/fist pump kind of motion showing sarcasm. She was trolling me before trolling was even a thing. "It's a big job."

She didn't have to say that last part. It was July Fourth weekend, and many of my friends and their families were cooking out or at the beach. Non-farm people had plans. We had work. It was tedious and boring and seemed to never end.

I grunted and retrieved old lawn chairs out of the storage building for us to sit in. A few were the old plastic-band straps that have metal arms and fold up. I didn't like them and opted for a wooden kitchen chair that's been relegated to the porch because it has seen better days. I was told to "stop riding it" — rocking it back on the hind legs — at least half a dozen times throughout the day.

Jane and I shucked corn for hours. Her boys played in the yard and I envied them. My mama shucked until the first bushel was done and then she went in the house to start the process that continued long past the expiration of daylight, well into the long, hot nights.

The shucking wasn't so bad, it was the silking I hated — pulling every last one of those hair-like strings off the cob took forever and leaving too much brought a reprimand. Later, we bought some stiff silking brushes, and they were welcome, but didn't completely relieve the misery. Adding to the toil was that some ears were damaged by insects, might have worms, or worse "cancer," which was actually a blue fungus. As a child, it was a mysterious and dangerous disease not to be touched.

We always planted yellow corn, the kind with big, juicy kernels, perfect for eating on-the-cob and easy to trim off for freezing. That used to be what everyone planted, but now, white or "silver" types seem to be the most widely available. I don't know why, because they definitely don't taste as good.

Daddy always disappeared somewhere and to this day I don't know where, but he did not shuck corn. Every eye on the stove was covered with a giant canning or soup pot with steam rising and the heat caused sweat to pour off all in the room, to be wiped with the back of a forearm or maybe a dish towel. Ear after ear was blanched — boiled and then dumped into a cold water/ice bath. These women of my family took butcher knives that look straight out of horror movies and shaved kernels off the ear into a big pan, long sheets of yellow sliding off, then a flick backwards on the cob to get the last bits, wasting none. Time was given to cool before they stuffed the vegetable gold into Ziploc bags and placed in the freezer. After a five-gallon bucket was full of cobs, I took them and dumped them in the field, where night critters would take them away and the leavings would rot into the soil, enriching the ground for the next year's crop.

There was always about a year's worth and then some for each of my siblings' families. Even though my brothers and sisters had all married and moved out to their own homes, my parents still planted a garden to feed a family of seven instead of the three still living in the house. I grumbled and complained about this a lot because there were things I had in mind to do. There were books from the bookmobile to finish before the next run. At our house, though, there was always something to read, like the newspaper, which brought the world to us every day and was considered a household essential in rural Nash County in the 1970s and 80s. I read it cover to cover and particularly enjoyed state columnist Dennis Rogers and was just getting into syndicated writer Lewis Grizzard, who was the first I remember to opine about Southern and redneck culture as a positive and definitely humorous subject. Those were the writers who made me think someday I might want to do what they're doing. I wanted to play ball. I wanted to do anything but work in the garden.

But corn was the job at hand.

• • •

My daddy had me put the wooden bushel baskets in the back of his pickup and then I climbed into the cab. Sometimes Mama would go on the short ride down Highway 97 to Edward Bissette's cucumber sorting shed. The tin-roofed shed shielded workers — mostly migratory men and women from Mexico — from the sun as loads of cukes went onto a belt to be sorted by size so they could be sent to buyers. This collection was the first step in making sweet pickles.

Sometimes Mr. Bissette was there, but often not and somehow Daddy managed to communicate with the foreman that was there for some cucumbers, even though he didn't speak a word of Spanish and I never heard any English from the workers. They always looked dead serious. I fetched the baskets and in no time a couple of workers had them filled and watched me struggle to get them back on the truck bed, grinning at my surprising lack of strength that did not match my size. I never remember seeing cash change hands, so I don't know what the arrangement was. Mr. Bissette was renting the bulk of my parents' farm, so later I figured that cukes and sweet potatoes were maybe part of the deal. I overheard enough at home to know the rent didn't amount to much — it might have been enough to cover the property taxes.

Once we got home, my job was to dig the stone crocks out of the storage building and hose them out. I put them up sparkling clean every summer. The crocks seemed like something from another century, old weathered, heavy, and dependable. Soon enough they'd be filled with cucumbers and covered in a brine of salt and water. There were several cycles. I asked Mama about the process not long ago, but it's been so many decades, and so much work has passed through her hands and so much worry through her mind, she couldn't remember exactly. There was a seven-day soak, then they were rinsed, put back in the brine with alum to crisp them up and then that was dumped for yet another rinse and soak with vinegar and sugar.

I didn't play close attention because I never felt like I'd be making pickles or want to. I was the crock dumper and I do have clear memories of that.

We had a yard, not a lawn. Lawns were for fancy town people. However, Daddy thought a lot of his yard.

"Dump them pickles for your mama," he'd say, gruffly. "And don't spill none of that shit in the yard. It kills the grass."

Now the grass that time of year was often — like mine is now — a combination of fescue, dandelions, and wire grass. And it only took a drop to kill a large spot. The crocks were heavy and if I sloshed any or stopped to re-grip and splashed any out, within a week I'd be convicted sure enough with a telltale brown ring in the yard. This would bring profanity, although no other real consequences. Looking back, we should have bottled that brine and used it as organic weed killer around the yard and garden, if only organic had been a thing. The stuff was potent. I even joked about it.

"Wonder what it does to your insides if it kills grass like that."

"For somebody so smart, you sure can be a dumbass," Daddy said.

Once the wonders of fermentation had walked through those crocks, the pickles were poured into quart Mason jars and put up in the pantry. Rows and rows of pickles that a reasonable person would never expect might ever be eaten. That changed once a reasonable person ate one on the side of a supper dish, or had them chopped up into the best potato salad in the world, or slapped onto a just-grilled hamburger. Every once in a while Mama would open a jar and inform me they'd "gone bad," but it was rare for a loss. The supply usually ran out about a week or two before the next summer, when the cycle would start again. There isn't a pickle on a grocery store shelf that is anywhere close to tasting like those sweet crunchy treats and I haven't had one in a long time.

• • •

Corn might have been the worst job, but it came and went in a week or two. It was the beans and peas that seem to go on forever. Part of the problem was that I loved corn, but had no taste for butter beans (lima beans to some), snaps (string beans to some), garden peas, and black-eyed peas that my family seemed to have an insatiable appetite for, so there was no payoff to consider while toiling down a row. In my later teens, when Mama rediscovered an old pepper relish recipe that would have made grass clippings edible, there was some comfort to be had. I hated the bending and crouching and picking and pulling and making sure the hulls were filled out. People now have the good sense to take a stool out to their gardens, but we had none of that softness in our world. Stools would have slowed the process and maybe even made you forget that the garden was work.

Like corn, I could not fathom why my folks planted so many rows of beans and peas. I think it must have even amazed them sometimes, because I remember a couple of years when we had so much produce, my parents called around to grocery stores to sell the excess. I do not know what they made, but I can remember going to small grocery stores in Nashville and Rocky Mount and seeing very happy men pass cash money to my mama as we dumped butter beans and snaps into containers in the back of the store, the heat still held in the hulls as the produce manager ran his hands through them like sand.

While I didn't much care for beans, there was a social aspect to preparing them that's gone away. Shelling was done on the porch until it got dark or the mosquitoes ran us inside. There was time to talk and listen, and even when we went inside to finish while watching TV, that was background noise. Friends or neighbors who stopped by would grab a pan while they were there and help shell while they visited, expecting nothing in return, knowing the favor would be returned if the roles were reversed. They talked about what was going on in the community. It helped me forget about how my fingers burned under the nails from shelling and if I had any slight cuts on my hands, they'd burn as well. Hands would be sore by bedtime, but at least it allowed me to watch Monday Night Baseball to the end more than once.

When it was done or when the tomatoes or squash piled up high enough and it was time to can, there were more sounds in the house. Quart Mason jars lined the table and once filled with tops and rings in place, would start popping in the afternoon, well into the night, a cacophony that signaled success and reassurance that the work was good.

• • •

Once, when I was really young, Daddy loaded the back of his pickup with baskets of all kinds of stuff. It was announced we were going to the Raleigh Farmer's Market where we could supposedly get a good price for all of it. It must have been about 1976 or so because I remember riding in Mama's lap, with her and one of my sisters stuffed in the cab. When we pulled into the parking lot, it was chaos. Daddy disappeared to find someone in charge. Going to Raleigh was something we did twice a year in those days, once to buy school clothes and then again for Christmas shopping. Now, many from our area drive to work in Raleigh every day. But it was a big deal then.

Everything seemed big and oversized and I distinctly remember staring at the tables mounded with tomatoes and melons and squash. I'd never seen so much produce in my life at one time. Things were all shapes and sizes and colors and there were vegetables I'd never seen. I wondered where our booth was going to be and how we'd even squeeze into one.

"Alright, let's go home," Daddy said.

"But we just got here."

"We ain't got nothing to sell," he said. We all looked at him and then saw a couple of men grabbing our vegetables out of the back of the truck. Someone bought it all before we could even pay for a booth. I'm not sure I saw him smile that big many times over the next 40 years, but he did that day with some cash in his pocket. Mama insisted that we at least walk through and see the spectacle, "the craziness," she called it. We did for a few minutes, but then the crowds were too much. I don't remember much else other than Daddy being coaxed into driving over to Peace Street so we could take home Krispy Kreme doughnuts. Crème-filled doughnuts seemed more than a fair trade for butter beans.

• • •

Many times in my youth I questioned why my parents spent so much of their time and effort in the field. Daddy had a "town job" by that point, managing a welding supply store in Rocky Mount. After working briefly at the local high school cafeteria, Mama, who could have stayed busy just running the household, started her bake shop, and it was growing. Only later would I understand that while economics played a role, raising food was more than that. It was in my family's DNA and had been ground into those helixes for centuries.

Both of my parents grew up during the last years of the Depression and during World War II rationing. This era dictated my grandparents' thoughts and behaviors for their rest of their lives, so it was no choice for them. Mama and Daddy grew up on farms, and not unlike all their neighbors, raised almost all their food — pork, chickens, beef, lamb, vegetables, fruit. They only needed the local store for things like sugar and tea and syrup. It was a different life.

By the time I was in high school, the number of friends on a farm or with sizeable gardens went from almost all to just a few. No longer did some classmates not show up for class until mid-September, when the last of the tobacco was curing, the barns humming in the night throughout the county, the sweet smell as comforting as the crickets, all composing a country lullaby for the senses.

·   ·   ·

One job I didn't mind, but would never have admitted it publicly, was digging sweet potatoes. It always seemed like they were planted in the worst soil in the garden, where it transitioned from the dark, warm, rich dirt to the harder, reddish clay our corner of the county was known for, the part of the garden nearest to the road.

It didn't take many sweet potato plants to get a big yield as the vines run and root. We always had a couple of long rows. They aren't hard to grow, but they do not tolerate cold weather, so we'd always "dig" ours long before the first frost so as not to take chances on losing this staple. I was glad to do this because it was and still is my favorite vegetable. Harvest always brought on an argument with my parents.

"Tonight after supper, we're going to get up sweet potatoes," my daddy would announce on a cooling September afternoon.

"Let us pull them up," my mama always said.

He'd grunt something and then go get the Farmall out with the smaller plows. He was determined to get as much tractor time as possible every year. This aggravated my mama to no end.

"Teeney, you will cut them all up," she said. "There ain't no need to waste all those potatoes." She won many arguments, but never ones that involved the tractor.

It would have taken longer and required more digging to pull up the vines, but it was not bad work. Daddy was pretty good with the tractor, but it was true, we lost many tubers to the blade. If they were big, we threw them into another basket for immediate eating. The others went in baskets to go to the storage building or in a bumper crop year, the old tobacco barns where they'd cure, the starches turning to sugar and making them even better.

Many times — often when another farmer or friend would come over — my daddy would go to the storage building and grab a handful of sweet potatoes or send me to fetch a couple and run into the house to get the salt shaker. He and the visitor would wipe them off, draw their pocket knives, cut thick slices and eat the potatoes raw like chips. It sounds awful, but actually was not bad. I'd usually eat a few pieces to impress the old men.

My favorite way to have them was when Mama started with the cut ones, careful to trim around the damaged areas, and make home fries in her old black cast-iron skillet lubricated with Crisco. They were crunchy on the outside and sweet and creamy on the inside. She also made turnovers, and we had baked sweet potatoes, custard pie, and casserole.

However, the greatest of all sweet potato recipes was the sliced pie. The potatoes were sliced and boiled and then laid into a pie crust. Some of the water was poured over the top and then lemon juice, sugar, allspice, and brown sugar were added before it was topped with another layer of crust. The leavings from the pot were seasoned for a juice that was poured over the pie when it was served. I've had a lot of desserts in my life, but nothing from any kitchen or bakery can touch it. I've seen no one else make it the same way outside my family and know the recipe came from my maternal grandmother. I've always assumed it was a product of her Depression ingenuity and creativity. She was the most practical woman I ever knew, and she had a sweet tooth (I wrote about her tea cookies in *Memory Cards*). The closest I could ever find online was a pie made similarly, but with molasses between the layers.

My county is the sweet potato capital of the world, growing and shipping all over the globe. I don't know why we don't have a festival, but that's kind of how this place is — do the work and keep your head down. It's hard to beat a good sweet potato.

•   •   •

There was always something to do from last frost to first frost every year. Something was always being planted or chopped or fertilized or watered or picked. We grew lettuce, cabbage, turnips (and turnip salad or the tops), squash, broccoli, cauliflower, eggplant, tomatoes, Irish (pronounced "eyesh") or "new" potatoes, mustard greens, onions, and even carrots a time or two. The bounty on the summer and fall table was impressive and there were many things we had almost every night that I didn't give a second thought to and now miss, like freshly sliced cucumbers and green onions soaked in vinegar with salt, pepper, and tomatoes done the same way. Squash and green tomatoes, and even eggplant during a couple of years of experimentation, were lightly battered and fried. Supper was a feast every night, a meat-and-three or four or even five sometimes, for no special reason. It was what came out of the field. It seemed at the time it would be like that forever and now it seems like that was forever ago. It's not coming back.

•   •   •

Corn out of a can is bland. The frozen product has no taste or is over seasoned with something exotic or far removed from the Southern palette as not to be accepted to the tongue. A bag from the grocery store that had grill marks on the kernels and was labeled "Mexican street corn," which sounded very inviting once lured my wife. It was an insult. Even small farmers and farmer's market vendors have strayed from what I remember as homegrown corn, big ears the length of a dinner plate, with big juicy yellow kernels. I feel like those days when I complained, I know Mama answered with "you might not have this one day" or "when you're grown you might not have a garden, you'll miss it and wish you had it." Miss the work? I was counting on it. I didn't know how prophetic she'd be.

What my folks did was thankless work that I didn't say ever say thanks for—I didn't appreciate it like I should have. I complained a lot and in my youthful naivete did not realize it was the best food I'd ever eat. I didn't have a canned or frozen vegetable until I was in college and like the big hair band Cinderella crooned in the 80s, you don't know what you got 'til it's gone.

7
No More to the Lake

The billboard that read "Langston's" was sun-bleached, paint-chipped and showing its age, but it was beautiful to me. It meant the long ride, painfully extended by youthful anticipation and the fact that most of it was on N.C. Highway 701, a tedious two-lane, was finally over.

As soon as we could unpack the car, I'd be set free to splash and swim in the cool refreshing waters of White Lake, just a few strides of my long preteen legs from the front door of the cottage.

August was a rough month in eastern North Carolina, as it was all over the South. Temperatures meant nothing; every day was a miserable, humid test of endurance until the sun went down. The garden was just past its peak, the tobacco harvest — at least for my family — was nearly done, and the beginning of a new school year was close at hand. All of that would be forgotten just as soon as I got a running start and jumped off the end of the pier.

As miserable as the dog days could be, this one last marker of the summer made those days bearable. I know I drove my parents and everyone else in the old grey-and-faux-wood paneled Mercury station wagon crazy.

"The ditches are getting sandy!" I'd shout as we started passing the roadside vegetable stands that served as landmarks.

"It won't be long," Mama would say.

At that point, I'd put my copy of *The Sporting News* or whatever James Bond novel I'd brought along on the seat, as if my vigilance would get us to our destination any quicker. Once we made that last turn, it was almost time.

Mama, who tried not to dampen my enthusiasm, endured it. "Start looking for water," she'd say. "We are almost there."

Once my folks checked in at the office, I'd hustle to do my share to lug those clunky blue vintage 1960s suitcases and the big red Coleman cooler inside. It took a lot of stuff to sustain a family on vacation, more so than I'd ever realize until I became a parent. As soon as everything from the car was in, I was immediately in a bathroom stripping down, and before that spring-triggered screen door could finish banging against its jamb, I heard, "Stay where I can see you! Don't get in over your head! Stay out from under the pier! Get out of there if you get cramps, you can drown that way! I will be right behind you!"

"I'll do my best not to drown," I'd yell back, laughing, dodging partially hidden tree stumps, kicking up sand, on my way to making sweet memories.

• • •

There were signs that read "The Nation's Safest Beach" at White Lake, a reassurance to Mama, who feared a great number of things that might happen to her children, from abductions to all sorts of freak accidents with garden implements — "Don't play around with that hoe, the next thing you know, you're going to rupture yourself!" White Lake is so named for its white sandy bottom and that gently slopes toward the center. There are no undercurrents and no sudden drop offs, and no harsh breakers, just gentle slapping waves sent shoreward from boats and jet skis operating in the deepest areas. The water was so clear that I could stand at any depth and see the bottom, just like a swimming pool. That was at least true to just over six feet, the height I stood the last year we went, just after my freshman year at Barton College. In Mama's mind, the lake was no death trap like the dangerous, crowded ocean beaches.

Mama never learned to swim and feared the undertow of the ocean. She stood a slender 5'2, with a dry sense of humor and a cautious eye for any number of life's pitfalls. We lived in a house where three girls had lived who drowned in the Tar River on a scorching afternoon 50 years earlier after getting caught in a mysterious whirlpool known as the Indian Hole, and this heightened her anxiety. In practice, she was terrified of most all bodies of water, so much so that despite living only a couple of hours from the Outer Banks, we never went to the beach until my late teens. It was the way she and most of her peers were raised in rural eastern North Carolina — the world outside the community was full of danger. But Mama was okay with White Lake — there was no riptide or sharks, and she could keep an eye on us. There was lots of sandy beach, and it was cheap enough to stay on the waterfront in a cottage with a kitchen and enough room to sleep all seven of us and then some. Looking back, it is funny how much she enjoyed those trips, even though she worked just as hard on vacation as she did at home — preparing three meals a day for the family, making sure we were stocked with supplies, and keeping the cottage clean.

My family started going to White Lake in the 1960s before I was born, learning of the place because of the Future Farmers of America camp there and from people at church who gave it high marks as family-friendly. My earliest memories are of us only staying for a weekend, but when my parents got out of farming and Daddy took an office job in Rocky Mount at a welding supply company, trips got extended to a week. We always stayed "on the water" because ironically, what was the point of going to the lake if you couldn't see it, mama always said.

My four brothers and sisters went — all adults by the time I was eight — sometimes for the entire week, sometimes for just a couple of days. They'd all married while I was still in elementary school, and so wives and husbands, and later, babies, added to the mix, although to me it never seemed crowded. Sometimes a cousin my age would tag along and we'd spend the days digging in the sand and seeking relief from the sun under the piers.

• • •

There were rules, but I never recall hearing them being spoken. There was little TV to be watched, except to get the weather in the morning, and maybe the news at night. The rabbit ears only pulled in about four channels anyway, so it wasn't much of a distraction. There was no alcohol involved. I don't know if anyone in my family drank then, but we were Baptists, so it would have been a secret, anyway. There was no smoking, although sometimes an invited "outsider" — a friend of my parents or siblings who might stay a day or two — would pull out a pack of cigarettes back when people didn't ask permission to light up. Another interesting fact that underlined the importance of this annual sojourn was that we usually left on a Sunday morning, significant because we never, ever skipped church, except when we went to White Lake.

• • •

White Lake is a geological anomaly known as a Carolina Bay. Geologists aren't positive, but believe meteorite crashes formed Carolina Bays. The lake is said to be clear because underground springs feed it. Although these bodies can be found from Georgia to Maryland, 800 of the 900 remaining are in North Carolina. There used to be thousands. White Lake is in Bladen County, near Bladen Lakes State Forest, between Elizabethtown and the port city of Wilmington. It seemed like such a paradise to me, but now I realize that area was more poverty-stricken than my county. Even the resort areas seem humble compared to the pristine condition of vacation condos and hotels people expect at coastal resorts today.

Carolina Bays are oval or round, mostly grouped on either side of the North Carolina-South Carolina border and many are now bogs or no longer hold water. At its deepest point, White Lake is 10 to 15 feet, depending on whom you ask. Its first appearance on a map was in 1770 when it was called Granston Lake. It became Bartram after that, and then got the name that stuck in 1886 because of the clear water and white, sandy bottom. The first public area opened as Melvin's Beach on the south side in 1901 and 20 years later Crystal and Goldston beaches — names that still carry water in the area — began operation. The next year, 1922, saw improved roads into the area which immediately created a tourist attraction. A series of glass-bottom boats patrolled the lake and the tour guide's voice over the PA system could be heard all the way to shore.

There were some pretty cool legends that always seemed to come up on our trips. Supposedly, the inventor of 7up — or was it Sun Drop or maybe Dr. Pepper — lived right on the lake, just across from wherever we were staying, no matter what side of the lake we were on. There was also supposed to be a famous novelist who lived there, but I never could nail down who it was, elusive as Robin Masters. And of course, there were many legends about disfiguring boat accidents that usually involved a lightning strike, a teenager and an explosion, but I always felt like my brother Bill made those up for Mama's benefit.

• • •

Cypress trees ringed the lake, partially in the water, hanging full with Spanish moss. Lapping, rhythmic waves, muffled the screams and squeals of children and admonitions from parents to stop running on the pier or to stop splashing a little brother or sister in the face. Entire days were spent in the water. It was a relief, a respite from life's demands. After a summer of heat and labor, it wasn't just about cutting loose, everyone exhaled. I swam and pretended my floats were battleships, like the USS North Carolina, which was harbored just down the road in Wilmington. There were constant water gun fights, but before the week ended, the weaponry would be ruined, fouled by the fine white sand. "Chicken fights" got out of hand and usually ended up with my sunning sisters and sisters-in-law getting splashed and exaggerating anger and seeking revenge.

Nights meant playing War or Monopoly or Hearts or Rook, as I soaked in family stories about long-passed relatives handed down on the screened-in porch that was standard for every cottage. Jokes were corny and sometimes racy, and always in plentiful supply, as was gossip. It always rained at least one day and one night, but never more. Nothing set the senses alive more than the tangy scent of rain filtering through the Spanish moss-covered trees in the yard, tapping a melody on the sheet metal roof, background music to the laughter and teasing and love that blew out into the late nights. Other vacationers often swam late into the night, with just enough illumination from the pier lights—you could hear the laughing and flirting and roughhousing drift across the still waters, as boats and jet skis were now docked at nightfall. I never went on those night dips, that time belonged to my siblings and their spouses.

It was thrilling to stay up with the adults and be un-policed on bedtimes. When the last of the card players or revelers called it quits, I'd put my book aside and sleep came easily to the drone of the cooling window unit air conditioner.

Things we didn't do at home, or have the time to do, we did. It was like we became another family, one without so much responsibility, without so much hard work, without livings to be made. This was a different life, a week, a vacation in the truest sense. It was an escape, but not from the people we loved and spent so much time with. I never sat on the porch at home and watched a thunderstorm pass or listened or carried on with others for hours—I always had something else to do. Not White Lake, though. Such a state of bliss seems elusive now.

• • •

Food was a big deal, and we cooked all of our meals at the cottage. In nearly 20 years of those trips, I remember us eating out once. A trip to the IGA, the only local grocery store around, brought back a week's smorgasbord. Breakfast meant bacon or sausage and eggs and toast. Lunch was usually a quick sandwich, just something fast so we could get back in the water—but not until we let our food settle for an hour (those dreaded cramps and/or drowning would descend, otherwise). I never realized until I was an adult that the settle time neatly coincided with how long it took my mother and sisters Jane and Carol, who were like second and third mamas, to cook and clean up the mess we all made. Daddy, who rarely cooked at home except on the weekends, fired up the charcoal grill almost every night, standing watch in a ribbed, sleeveless t-shirt, dress pants, and bare feet. His specialty was barbecued chicken, and he was known for his sauce or "hot ton" (rhymes with John), a mixture of vinegar, ketchup and spices that was legendary among neighbors and friends back home. My favorite was hamburgers cooked on the grill with a big slab of hoop cheese or the plasticky yellow slices, topped with a mound of "husky mix" — chopped lettuce, sweet pickles, and onions, bound with Catalina dressing.

One night, usually Friday or Saturday, we walked to the pavilion on the trail that encircled the entire lake. The pavilion was a madhouse of people, so many, so loud, playing games to win prizes and the approval of newfound beach romances. Bells clanged, pinball machines rattled and blinked, and the air was hazy and heavy with popcorn and tobacco smoke. There was the constant traffic of stuffed animals and warped, elongated soft drink bottles, string art, and Budweiser beach towels paraded about. Just before we got there, we passed through the "black part" of the Lake. While government imposed, legal segregation was long gone in the 1970s and 80s, there was still a separation of the races, each seemingly too busy enjoying the water or the pinball machines to take note — but I know now that they did. As a child, it puzzled me how this worked.

Putt-Putt was important and took on a competitive edge, but win or lose, it ended with a stop at the walk-up Dairy Queen for hot fudge sundaes. This was the only DQ I knew of, exotic beyond the Tastee Freezes back home. And, there was always a pass through the gift shops filled with water guns, rafts, and knickknacks and plaques, all emblazoned with White Lake, N.C. in script and some corny joke. I did not imagine there was another place in the world to vacation or that these trips would ever end.

• • •

Eventually, jobs got more demanding, the family moved away from farming, and my siblings' families grew, and vacation times were determined by bosses. It was nearly impossible to find a house big enough to accommodate a mushrooming family, and that was the whole point of the trip, being together. I couldn't imagine what those who didn't go could possibly be doing that they would miss the highlight of the year. What could be better?

White Lake started having troubles of its own about the same time. The last year we went, water levels were low and the previously crystal clear water was dark green and murky. Many of the cottages were in disrepair, showing their age, holes in the roof, evidence of mice and insects.

We skipped a year, that year turned into a decade, and before we knew it, our family vacations were over and we never took another one, an unceremonious end to a tradition we all thought would last forever.

"We'll go back next year," became "We need to go again one year" to "I miss going to White Lake" to "Remember when we used to all go to White Lake?"

Little did we know it was foreshadowing for the day when holidays would send us into rotating years of family gatherings, and those gatherings would mostly fall by the wayside as well. Change never seems to give fair warning.

• • •

Mama always wanted a big family, but that growth was the undoing of White Lake trips, and honestly, other family gatherings as well. Our streak of get-togethers was so impressive, that when it abruptly ended, I explained it to Mama this way:

"Mama, we have to look at this thing like we got away with it for a long time. We dodged bullets for years that other families didn't."

The closeness of gatherings can't be sustained when a family reaches a certain population density. That's no criticism of the people and I only now have come to understand and appreciate how well everyone got along in those close quarters, especially when this was the same group of people we spent the rest of the year with. Eventually, some were too far-flung, too different, babies grown up with families of their own, too many obligations and interests and jobs and finances.

That last year we went is a good example. My two brothers-in-law, both of whom I loved like brothers, and I drove from White Lake to nearby Whiteville to play golf. We had so much fun, we said we should make it an annual thing. We never went again. Eventually, one would leave the family in divorce and the other would pass away, years before he should have.

• • •

Like most people fortunate enough to grow up in a large family, I took those trips and big meals for granted. Now they've all but disappeared. At times they seemed overwhelming, as if there was no chance at a new adventure during certain times or holidays in the year.

There was my Aunt Vannette's Christmas Eve dinner and Granny's Christmas Day, the former ending with a premature passing, the latter due to age finally taking its toll. Then there was the weekly meal at my parents' house. Every Sunday after church, my brothers and sisters and nephews and nieces gathered for a massive lunch. Saturday nights before I was born was usually dinner and pro wrestling I was always told, and later it was burgers or steaks on the grill. As a teenager, I wanted to escape this and go get fast food with my friends, true evidence of an empty brain in those days. Even on Friday nights, some family would come over for supper, and then stick around for "The Dukes of Hazzard" and "Dallas."

We still have Thanksgiving and Christmas get-togethers, but because the family is so large, someone is always in a rotation with other family. Even the more recent tradition on my wife's side of meeting at the beach for Thanksgiving supper and weekend has ended. There have been deaths and divorces and now, even the great-grandkids of my parents have married off.

When I was younger, I figured I'd take my future wife and our family on those White Lake trips. But the trips ended before we got together. She would have loved it.

Oddly, we've never talked about going. Of course, we wouldn't have the same experience. I'm sure everything would seem smaller or less exciting. I don't know what the water is like, but it could never be as clear as my memory says it was. Our kids would miss the sea shells and waves they love so much at the beach.

There wouldn't be the buzzing, crowded kitchen or the hotly contested card games.

I imagine the water is too shallow for a grown man to get a running start and jump off the end of the pier, probably not for my teenage children, either. And even if it was, it wouldn't be the same lake I remembered, my old friend. My family doesn't have a White Lake. We don't go to the same place two years in a row, much less 25.

The place I so naively thought would always be there is a distant memory. What was a constant, precious thing is gone. It never was about the lake though. While it was beautiful and fun, we had all we needed before we left home.

We could drive back to the lake, but we can't go back. My brothers and sisters and I just have those perfectly formed memories that still make us stop and smile and remember for a moment before gently fading like the late August Carolina sun.

8
Homemade Ice Cream

It's a fading Sunday afternoon in the second half of the summer. The temperature is surely in the high 80s, but no one can confirm as there are no cellphones or 24-hour news and the old Texaco thermometer that used to hang on the tobacco barn is long gone. It doesn't matter so much because the century old pecan trees offer plenty of shade, a canopy over our backyard.

Lunch is hours past, but most of the adults are still recovering from the week's stuffing at the gathering that takes place once all my brothers and sisters and their families have made their way out of church and to my mama's table. She's made all the favorites to go with my daddy's famous barbecued chicken that he cooked on the grill while everyone else sat through sermons. Daddy didn't go to church.

I've hassled my brothers and brothers-in-law to play basketball or baseball, a plea I make every week with good results. No one is having any of it today as they shoo flies and gnats and fan themselves every so often with a wave of their hands. Then someone makes a suggestion.

"Why don't we make homemade ice cream?"

This causes a stir. "Yeah, why don't we?" I hear my mama say, and that's followed by murmurs and various personal colloquialisms of agreement. The group at the picnic table stirs into action, those in lawn chairs rising from the metal and strap in search of the ice cream maker, and the tub. The men discuss who is going to run to the store for a couple of bags of ice and a box of rock salt. No one keeps rock salt around here because you only need it scatter on the steps when it snows or when someone strikes a notion to make ice cream — both events coveted and rare jewels.

Mama goes to make sure there's enough sugar and milk around. Homemade ice cream is simple, if not labor intensive in early 1980-something. I'm excited, because we hardly ever make ice cream and it is the best thing on earth to eat. Later, I'll question if it was so good because we hardly ever made it or because it really is the best thing on earth. I realize I'm going to be mostly a spectator or go-fer in this operation, so I make a suggestion.

"Let's make strawberry! Can we make strawberry?"

I know I'm not going to make headway on the flavor. Everyone in my family loves strawberries, but they are no longer in season. Instead, many pints and quarts have been frozen and stashed in my parents freezer in the storage building for the fall and winter. We've finished our picking from the local farms, a flurry of trips late in the day over a couple of weeks. The strawberry binge is over. We've had them chopped (with sugar added) and dumped onto homemade cakes, those little cupped cakes that come in six packs, with Twinkies, baked into cakes, and as topping for cream cheese and Cool Whip based pies. And then we don't touch them again until cold weather comes and we can "reach in the freezer and pull out the garden in the winter when we really need it," Mama always says.

I know we won't be making strawberry. We never do. The die is already cast.

"Peach. How about peach?" someone asks. Everyone agrees because they all know it's the correct answer.

We always make peach for a couple of reasons: one, they are in season and there are plenty of peach orchards around us. Two, peaches are cheap. Three, part of the reason of making homemade ice cream is to get something you can't get at the store. In our corner of the world, the store has just a couple of ice cream flavors in my childhood: vanilla, chocolate, neopolitan, and chocolate swirl. You certainly can't buy peach and while you can get strawberry, it's artificial with no fruit chunks in it. I don't offer much of a protest. I like peach fine, but I have to make the case for something else, because this is a rare occasion might be repeated once more before the summer ends if we're lucky.

The women are inside, pulling chopped peaches from the fridge — a trip to Finch's or Bissette's orchards had been made earlier in the week and after peeling and pitting and chopping and sugaring, the peaches are ready for the freezer, joining others in pink plastic containers with clear lids, stacked neatly alongside the strawberries.

Chairs will need to go to the backyard, a job that mostly falls to me. Some lawn chairs appear from the packhouse and I bring out some of the more worn inside chairs from the kitchen and porch. The shade and breeze and anticipation of ice cream will bring a welcome relief from the sweltering late summer afternoon sun.

There is talk and laughter and daredevil dragonflies and anticipation as the adults wring out the last bit of the weekend before work resumes the next morning. No one is thinking about work right now, just funny stories, most from before I was born, things that happened in the fields or at work or most often, pranks pulled on each other, friends, enemies, or classmates. Sometimes there's gossip, sometimes there are jokes, sometimes there are just pauses and for a few seconds, there is only the squeak of the chains that hold the swings. Plans for the future are made, next week and next year and in a little while or in a few years or the often used, vague and wistful term, "before I die," as in "I sure do want to see the Grand Canyon before I die."

• • •

Soon, it's all coming together, the action reaching a climax. The men are back, laughing, carrying bags of ice and a box of Morton's Rock Salt. The wooden tub is pulled out from the storage building and one of my sisters, Jane or Carol, has rinsed out the metal tank and plastic lid and the paddles that go inside. My brother-in-law Eddie goes inside to retrieve the tub, full with fruit and milk and sugar, and he lowers it in place. He and my brothers Bill and Jimmy layer the ice and rock and salt around the tank. My brother-in-law John is telling a story that he thinks is hilarious and it might be as we wait to see.

"Don't get salt in it," my daddy advises from the hammock. He'll say this a couple of more times as he watches carefully, wearing a white-ribbed undershirt, dark dress pants, and no shoes, his usual at-home uniform. Later, when the tank is removed from the tub, he'll offer the same advice, a little sharper as we all anticipate the cold, sweet taste of ice cream.

We're not there, yet, though and it's now time for the hard part. The hand cranking starts. I hope for a turn, but it will not be granted. I think it is because the adults think I can't do it. In the years to come, I eventually get my turn and the glamour and prestige of helping make the ice cream evaporates as quickly as the water in the tub. Soon, my shoulder burns from the repetitive cranking of the metal lever with the wooden handle, but really, it is the mental tediousness that is driving me crazy. I'm now bound to the top of the picnic table, unable to make the rounds to my family, to try to coerce someone to play or just listen in on what they are talking about.

Years later, Jane will get a fancy new electric ice cream maker. It plugs in and starts turning and other than making sure to layer in salt and ice, that's all that has to be done. In roughly the same amount of time, the ice cream is done — the machine magically knows when it is finished and shuts itself off. I think that we've hit the jackpot, that now we will make ice cream more often since we have eliminated the worst labor. I am wrong. At a larger function years later, I hear several older people say the ice cream is not as good made with the electric machines. I can't figure out how the ice cream knows the difference.

At long last, the ice cream is declared ready. My brother-in-law removes the crank and carefully lifts the tank out of the ice and water and salt mix among admonishments from others to be careful. He carefully takes off the white cap of the tank as everyone drifts towards the ice cream with bowl in hand. Carol appears with a soup ladle and starts dishing up the treat while everyone stares at the spoon, mesmerized at how in less than an hour all that soupy slosh has been coaxed into the world's best treat. Or maybe that's just me. Servings are modest at first to make sure everyone gets some. Soon, all that can be heard in the backyard is the sound of spoons clacking ceramic bowls and an occasional moan in appreciation of those who've made the ice cream, some suggesting ecstasy.

"This is so good."

"Mmm ... UMM!"

"Why don't we do this more?"

"Oh, the peaches are sweet this year."

"Mmm. Let's make some next Sunday."

"Let's make strawberry next time."

I try to make my bowl last, but too soon it's gone. I'm back in line for more, a couple of more spoonfuls. Homemade ice cream is only good fresh. It just doesn't store well in the freezer, not that we ever have any left that I can remember.

• • •

I still don't know why we didn't make ice cream more often. It really wasn't that much trouble. My wife and I have made it, but not very often and as I started writing this, I realize our maker stopped working years ago and we never replaced it. It seems like no one makes it very often now or in the past, but people love it and homemade ice cream is guaranteed to boost attendance at events when it is weaponized.

I know this because churches often used an "Ice Cream Supper" to promote the opening of bible schools or summer revivals or Sunday School attendance drives. Just the announcement of such an event brought involuntary moans in even the most conservative Baptist congregations of my youth. These events caused a buzz — ice cream for supper — it seemed a sinful notion, but was permitted. A dozen or more families would volunteer to make a tub, and this is where I learned there were other things out there besides peaches. I could always count on strawberry, but there would be chocolate and chocolate chip and vanilla and cherry. Someone made pineapple once and I distinctly remember seeing a green and an orange and a yellow, but these held no allure for me. It just reinforced my puzzlement of why we never made anything but peach other than once or twice.

• • •

Hurricanes have taken all but one of those grand old pecan trees in the last two decades, but it's been at least that long since we have made ice cream in my parents' backyard. As I grew up in the 1980s, those creamy Sunday afternoons became more and more rare. There was no peach ice cream sold in stores then or now, I suppose because of the trouble of peaches quickly turning brown if not preserved.

The Tastee Freeze in Bailey came up with a brilliant idea after they remodeled and went from strictly a drive-in to adding a nice large dining room. Besides offering the chain's standard fair, they started offering peach milkshakes made with local peaches while they were in season. This is my earliest memory of an "in season" promotion and it became my go-to treat after Friday night church league softball games. The Tastee Freeze was about the only show in town after dark and was the hangout for most every local teenager with a driver's license.

While my friends stuck with chocolate and vanilla, I went all in on the peach. It was a fair homage to homemade ice cream, and pretty soon, if anyone I knew was working, once I came in the door, they'd start my peach milkshake. They only lasted a few weeks, so I felt like I was on the clock. I had to remember to get a spoon if I was getting it to go, if there was riding around to do because there wasn't much else going on — which is why we played softball on Friday nights to begin with — because there would always be lots of cold chunks of peach to fish out at the bottom of the Styrofoam cup, one last taste of summer.

The Tastee Freeze is gone now, lost when a longtime employee bought it from the longtime owners and not so long after took her own life. It was tragic losing such a familiar, friendly face and an institution all at once. Later, it became a Hardee's. Now when I get a summer milkshake, it's usually from a local strawberry farm, and it's almost always strawberry, although I have to opt for the "no sugar added version." They don't have peach. Times have changed and so have I.

Today, Chick-Fil-A offers a peach milkshake for a brief time each year, which seems appropriate for a Georgia outfit. Cookout has one as well. There are both great. I rarely get one, maybe only as often as we made homemade ice cream, and the first taste often brings back, just for a moment, the backyard, the heat, and the laughter.

9
What I Like About Sundays

The piano player — it could have been any of the three or four ladies, well known, well-respected, counted on — fired up the first strands of the "Doxology." From the vestibule emerged four men, all faces I recognized, knew as leaders of the church. They stepped into the aisle in lockstep, felt-lined wooden offering plates in hand, full of fresh collections.

Praise God, from whom all blessings flow;
Praise Him, all creatures here below;
Praise Him above, ye heavenly host;
Praise Father, Son, and Holy Ghost. Amen.

As if practiced, the men turned after placing the plates on the altar, and eyes ahead, marched back down the aisle, the doors closing as the congregation reached "Amen." It's almost as if they trained Baptist men in timing to get this right. You'd think we'd be better dancers because of it.

The song and the closing of the doors were welcome to me. I slid off my ill-fitting loafers, always too short, or too narrow it seemed, never worn enough to break in, only out of the closet on Sunday mornings. Without asking or saying a word — because the preacher was already pacing through the scripture on which his sermon was based — I curled up on the pew. I twisted enough not to kick my sister and put my head in Mama's lap. We sat in the back righthand corner of the old church built in the 1920s, short rows of hard pews by the door, an area that could be closed off for Sunday

School or overflow nursery if needed, just a row or two behind the regular long pews in the sanctuary. There was a reason we always sat here, although I didn't know it at that the time. All I knew or cared about was that Mama's right hand would gently rest on my shoulder and she'd rub my hair until I fell asleep.

This worked even on the hottest summer days in the old clapboard building that had no air conditioning or when the wintry winds could be heard outside the stained glass windows, whipping and drafting a biting chill while the fire and brimstone projected from the pulpit. None of it mattered to me as I thought of the rest of the day, the part I liked about Sundays, just on the other side of this onrushing sleep.

•　•　•

My memory doesn't allow for many years of those Sunday morning naps. There were plenty of older men around me that drifted off as well, they just did it upright without the benefit of a loving mama's touch, only a wife with a well-placed elbow into the ribcage to prevent a waking jolt or worse, snoring.

There was never a question about whether our family was going to church on Sunday morning. The wake-up call came early. It was the one day a week Mama didn't cook breakfast, but that was because the stove and oven were fully involved for Sunday Lunch — very often snap (aka string bean) casserole (the kind with cream of mushroom soup and fried onions on top), corn pudding, butter beans, and if Daddy wasn't barbecuing chickens, a meat loaf, roast, or ham. My brothers and sisters were all at least 10 years older than me, so I mostly remember them rolling out for Sunday School in their cars, sometimes riding with us, sometimes picking up or riding with a date, but all dressed in Sunday clothes. This was what I hated the most. I was not yet showering in the morning and my straight, thick brown hair took quite a few pulls from a wet comb to be tamed into an acceptable presentation. There was the crisp white shirt and polyester pants and usually a clip-on tie. The slick, black socks were tight and left marks, but it was the shoes that were the worst.

• • •

Sometimes, one of us would claim to be too sick to go to church. The comfort of the bed, or the excitement of TV with no one else in the house but Daddy were real temptations. I never quite understood how he got a pass and didn't have to go to church.

"If you're too sick to go, you're too sick to play this afternoon." That was usually threat enough to suck it up.

"I want to watch TV. I don't feel like going to church," was to be met with something like "Well, it's a good thing God doesn't take a day off," or "You only have to go once a week." Southern mamas are well-skilled in guilt persuasion.

I didn't understand why we couldn't just stay at home some weeks, especially when it was raining hard or really cold or so hot. Later, I would understand Mama was forming habits for churchgoing in us, habits that have lasted all of her children and grandchildren for decades. She was adhering to the verse about raise up your children in the way they should go and they won't depart from it.

Sunday School started at 9:30 a.m. and was pretty fun when I was a child. We'd usually make something with glue and construction paper and hear a Bible story we'd heard over and over for years. It was my cousins and me and people I didn't realize were distant cousins, all raised in the small community where Mama grew up, about 15 minutes from where we lived. Sometimes there were cookies and Kool Aid. Mama taught my class until I was five, and raised generations of people in that class, serving until her late 70s, a good 50 years in the Wide Awakes class. In one of my later classes, a teacher would usually play the autoharp for us, an instrument I didn't really appreciate until later when I discovered the music of Mother Maybelle Carter.

Later I'd have a mix of teachers. Some were schoolteachers who felt like Sunday School should be no different from regular school. This made for miserable days, no talking, no socializing with others in class, just 45 minutes of well-meaning, hardcore, tuned out literature, sometimes just read aloud. Sermons often weren't much better.

But that changed when a younger man showed up to be pastor not long after I graduated from being able to sleep through the service. He had a daughter about my age and a knack for telling stories and making those familiar Bible passages seem relevant. He baptized me on a cold Sunday night in February 1978. I was almost nine.

•　•　•

As bad as it sounds, the highlight of Sundays for most of my youth came with the last "amen" after that last hymn, when the final faltering parishioner had come forward to the altar to pray or rededicate or request a baptism. I knew these were good things. But when we were done was the best.

The preacher lined up at the door to shake hands with everyone as they departed. We did that for years, and while there was probably never a Sunday that it took more than 15 minutes to empty the church, it seemed like forever. There was always some old woman talking about her corns or rheumatism or some old man making cringe-worthy jokes about his wife or complaining about the weather. Eventually, Mama, a natural introvert, found reasons to go back to her room for something she forgot or some other reason to slide out the side door or back door. We wasted no time getting home so she could finish lunch and get it on the table.

Pulling into the yard meant freedom unlike any other day of the week.

I'd push the door open sometimes before Mama could get the old VW van in park, pulling off my tie and unbuttoning my collar and then shirt, sometimes liberated from those awful clothes before I made it to my room. In no time I'd be in way too short early 80s shorts and white tube socks with three colored stripes at the top, pulled up to my knees, eagerly awaiting the arrival of my brothers and later brothers-in-law, who after the biggest meal of the week could usually be persuaded to play basketball or baseball or football or take me fishing in the pond across the road. There was no school, no homework, no chores.

The food was good and my entire family was always there, no more than one or two absences every few months. I thought it would always be that way.

• • •

As time passed and my brothers and sisters all married, had children, and some started going to church elsewhere, Sunday lunch evolved into more of a potluck. My sisters were exceptional cooks like my mama and while we could always count on Mama to provide traditional country cooking, my sisters often brought the exotic. There were casseroles and desserts like Mississippi Mud Cake and Strawberry Pie and baked beans and beefaroni.

After the big meal, I could hardly contain myself. North Carolina is known as Tobacco Road, where basketball is king, and then, like now, there is a hoop in most every yard. Basketball was always in season and usually from February to November — the dog days of July and August demanding the only break — I'd have my brother-in-law John showing me moves and working on my jumper and roughing me up and prepping me for later years when my house was the place to be on Sunday afternoons for all day 3-on-3 games. One reason was because my friends and I all lived for basketball, another was because my goal was on the side of a tobacco barn, with a hard-packed dirt surface. It didn't hurt much to fall, there was little chasing of errant shots and after about two o'clock, the barn offered some shade.

When it was too hot for basketball, we used the barns as outfield walls for wiffle ball and when it was cold, we went to my sister's house across the road for football. My buddies and I worked off our heavy meals — many of them had the same church and lunch traditions we did. It wasn't unusual because pretty much everyone went to church in those days, even the wildest Saturday night rounders.

Later, my nephews took my spot, and I elevated to the role that John had played, making teams and rules. We played all afternoon, every Sunday.

• • •

From the outside, those Sunday lunches might have seemed like they were about the food. Sometimes special guests would come over, like the preacher and his family. We almost always had Daddy's barbecued chicken on those days, crispy skin covering juicy meat, doused in a mild, but peppery red sauce that begged to be drizzled on everything on my plate and sopped up with Mama's homemade sourdough rolls.

As I became an adult, I was more excited about seeing family. After I married and Kristi and I started our family, the joy we could see when we brought kids in the door of my parents' house was obvious. They were passed around and loved, just like my nephews and nieces had been. The conversation that I paid little attention as a child — the community news, concerns at work, promotions, stories about co-workers, the latest plans at church, the latest gossip — became more important. And I thought those times would last forever, at least on some level I let myself think that, even though I had to know it wasn't true, it wasn't possible.

• • •

Eventually, I became a deacon in the church I grew up in. I learned that being an adult at church was surely not as easy as being a child. We had good times and bad and turmoil, just like any group has. Love that went beyond those differences kept things together, kept people serving.

Sometimes I didn't feel well and didn't go to church. Sometimes I just didn't feel like going. Sometimes I needed a break. Sometimes I just wanted to watch *CBS Sunday Morning* with North Carolina's Charles Kuralt and later, Charles Osgood. It was about arts and people and good stories and all the things I loved, a video magazine. Other people stayed home and read their thick newspapers and sometimes I wanted to do that, too.

I never outgrew the feeling I was doing something wrong when I didn't go.

• • •

Sunday Lunch started to slowly fade away. John passed away after an accident on a golf trip. My siblings' growing families fell into their own Sunday routines. Family members moved — some out of state, some out of country. Pretty soon we were down to fewer than 10 people and it became sort of overwhelming for my elderly parents. The tradition went out with a whimper, not a bang. It now takes a holiday to bring everyone together, and even then, usually someone is out.

I learned a lot from those meals. When someone offers you food, they are telling you a story — about themselves, your relationship, what they are like, how they grew up and where they are from. It's communication by sharing and sometimes it is a real test of friend-worthiness. Sharing a meal is not something owned by one culture, it links all cultures with a common bond, proving that a meal is a gift from creation and much more than sustenance and survival.

10
Hog Tied

I knew I was in trouble when I set the prongs on his testicles and pressed the button on the handle of the prod and nothing happened.

The next thing I knew, the boar slammed me against the railings, turned and lifted me off my feet. I crashed onto the concrete floor and banged my head. I don't remember if it was on the railing or the floor, I just remember struggling to get to my feet before the hog got turned all the way around. I weighed about 175 and he was easily twice that or more and a whole lot meaner, with sharp teeth and power.

We only used shock sticks as a last resort, and then only usually a light brush on the haunch unless an animal was about to hurt someone or another hog. Boars can be unpredictable and temperamental, especially when being separated from females.

Thankfully, when the flow of animals from one house to another stopped, my brother Bill came to see what the problem was, yelling and kicking with his steel-toed boots. By the time I got back on my feet and shook off the cobwebs, he'd relocated the animal and was back to check on me. At about roughly the time he determined I was okay, my brother started laughing.

•   •   •

Genealogy shows that both sides of my family have farmed dating back to at least the 1700s. Hogs were part of that equation since before the Civil War.

No close relatives are involved now and haven't been for decades. If any of those old timers were to time travel, I think they'd be shocked.

Not that hog farming was some grand tradition. It doesn't make my family special, since hog farming was pretty common in North Carolina, and although it has changed drastically, it is still a way of life for many. It took less property to raise hogs, and it is an animal where everything but the squeal can be brought to the table.

Bill took a couple of turns at it, the first being during my early teens when I was assigned as his workforce. Being a teenager on a hog farm is a shitty job, pun intended. But we were at the advent of the "modern age" of the business in the 1980s, so even though it was tough, it was a great deal better than previous generations had it.

For a kid who had no appreciation for farming of any kind, no desire for hard work, and certainly no love for working with livestock, it was a dreaded everyday affair. I've often joked than it was the motivation for me to attend college and served notice that not only did I not want to make a living with my hands, that I would likely have starved if it came down to that.

Hog farming was the last connection to earning any portion of a living from the land for my family. When I was a young boy, my parents raised tobacco, cows, chickens, and hogs. They sold excess vegetables raised on several acres to local stores and at the farmer's market. Eventually, Daddy turned to full-time work managing the office of a welding supply company and Mama's bake shop took off, so we cut back to a massive garden until Bill went into hogs.

Three structures were built on the farm, down a path past my brother's house, which was across the road from my parents. The entire farmstead was 30-some acres. One house was for sows (mother hogs to be), one was a nursery (for sows who had just given birth), and one was for pigs that had recently been weaned. Each house was long with a metal roof and concrete floor. The first one featured curtains on the sides of the house that could be raised in hot weather and lowered in cold weather. The second and third were enclosed, but with vented openings instead of windows. They all had fans, and the floor was sloped so that waste could be washed out by small dumpster-like containers on an axle that filled with water throughout the day before tipping over, sort of like those you see at indoor water parks now. The dumpsters dumped into a track that carried outside to a state-mandated lagoon, essentially a small pond several feet deep filled with hog excrement. One of my jobs every day was to get into the pens and shovel the rest of the manure into the track for washing out, and to use the water hose to help keep the pens clean.

There were silos in front of each building. I'd pull the metal chute over a wheelbarrow in that middle aisle and fill it with feed and walk down the length of the house filling the feed bins. The roar of the grunting hogs would start building as soon as I flipped the switch. It would get so loud, we couldn't even hear each other yelling — it was as if the animals hadn't been fed in days. There were several watering nipples in each pen, fed from PVC pipes overhead that gave the hogs access to water anytime they wanted it.

The fans ran all day in the summer and there were days I'd open the door and my glasses would fog with heat and humidity. After about late May, the curtains on the side stayed rolled up to allow air circulation, which helped with the temperature but did nothing for the odor.

Even after working in the hogs every day for years, I never did get over that smell. It somehow gets into the nostrils and stays and no amount of the nose blowing or showering can completely rid it. It settles on a hog farmer and reminds him he's in a dirty, thankless business.

• • •

Pork is a universally loved food, but it's safe to say its base is in the South. In North Carolina, barbecue means chopped shoulder meat that's been cooked over charcoal, wood, or gas and then seasoned. From the Raleigh-Durham area to the coast, that seasoning is red pepper and vinegar. Around the middle part of the state to the foothills, the seasoning is tomato based. As with all barbecue types, the rivalry is fierce. In South Carolina, the sauce is mustard based. Beware of imitators, especially "authorities" that appear on TV shows pontificating about "Carolina style" barbecue. That's your tipoff that they don't know what they are talking about because there are three distinct types in two states. These false prophets will tell you about shortcuts and "real" sauce and it usually involves a crock pot or ketchup. That's nonsense unless you think there is nothing special about Kansas City ribs, Chicago deep-dish pizza, San Francisco sourdough, or Vidalia onions.

Of course, we all favor what we're raised on, and for me that is good old eastern North Carolina barbecue. They serve the best examples in places like Sam Jones BBQ, Skylight Inn, B's and Bum's in Pitt County, near Greenville, the epicenter of eastern style barbecue: Parker's and Marty's in Wilson; Wilbur's in Goldsboro; King's in Kinston; Red Neck BBQ Lab in Benson; Old Colony Smokehouse in Edenton; or Doug Sauls in Nashville. Every town used to have a barbecue joint, but no longer. People expect fast food prices for this labor-intensive food. Many notable places that fed the population, places like Jack Cobb & Sons in Farmville, Bill's in Wilson, and Bob Melton's in Rocky Mount have closed, some for financial reasons, some because the family desire to carry the restaurant on no longer existed. Barbecue is served with simple sides — some form of cornbread, slaw, Brunswick stew[1], collards, baked beans, potatoes, string beans, and French fries. Most joints serve fried chicken, and some have barbecued chicken or ribs, as well as fried chicken livers and gizzards. Some have seafood — usually fried shrimp, oysters, and fish, sometimes only on a particular night.

Many of these places only take cash or check, and only a couple accept credit cards. Customers — even in this day and age of plastic and electronic money — will conform to the rules when the food is that good.

There is no real reason not to experience the best North Carolina has to offer. There have been countless books, lists, columns, magazines, TV stories, and maps produced about where to go.

---

[1] Brunswick Stew is a tomato-based dish, a cousin to homemade vegetable soup, except tremendously thicker. It usually has every vegetable from the canning or freezer - corn, butter beans, snaps, stewed tomatoes ... most people add stringed chicken, and some add hamburger or pork. [Very] old timers will say it has to have squirrel, but I never had it that way ... that I know of. It is seasoned very simply — salt, pepper, garlic and onion powder. One legendary master cook I knew was alleged to have used moonshine as a secret ingredient, but this was never verified.

There are other ways to get barbecue besides in one of these fine eateries. Many families own a whole hog pig cooker or have a pit in the yard for a pig pickin'. This is an event that is usually held to celebrate an accomplishment or an occasion — someone's birthday, wedding or anniversary, or the end of a long project, or to thank people who might have helped on the farm during the year, or to celebrate a holiday with the neighbors. When I was younger, a pig was separated from the others and fattened for several days. Now, folks can go to the local slaughterhouse or family-owned grocery and get a pig already split and dressed and ready for the cooker — it's best to arrive for transport in a pickup truck. I remember Daddy and my brothers got up before daybreak to start the pig, sitting around telling stories, talking trash, and flipping the pig every few hours. This included seasoning, and after several hours, nibbling at the meat. I often joked that I never knew a pig had ribs until I was an adult, because there was rarely any left by the time the meal was served.

Once the pig was done around suppertime, some was chopped and put in a serving bowl, but typically guests would step over to the cooker and pick what they wanted straight off the carcass. Some liked long pieces of stringy meat, some liked tenderloin, others wanted something with crispy skin. Whatever was left after the party was picked off and packed for the freezer.

• • •

I came home from school in the afternoons and took time to drink an Orange Crush or Mountain Dew and read the newspaper for a few minutes while grabbing a snack. If I was slow to come off this break, Mama would send me on my way soon enough, down the path to the hog houses.

Most days were about feeding and checking the water. This took time in the three houses. In the middle house, we kept sows and newborns in small confining chutes to keep the piglets and mothers close until weaning. They kept the sow from turning around to prevent hurting the piglets, but also to prevent her from going after anyone who tried to touch her babies. Never mind the cartoon images of hogs. They can and will hurt a person if provoked.

Working in the second house meant making sure it was relatively clean and monitoring the babies and mother for scours (aka diarrhea). These pens had to be hosed down every day and were kept hotter because of the babies. A sow can have a dozen or more piglets at the time and they had to be given shots. To understand how this worked, one might consider the old expression "slippery as a greased pig." In the old days, the "grease" was mud and feces. In modern hog farming it was just feces.

Shot day was not a day I looked forward to. Despite gotcha journalism stories, the health of animals has always been important to good farmers. Baby pigs got vaccines and let me tell you, it was not an easy job. It could actually be comical, but only if you were a bystander, not the person with the syringe or the piglet. This was chaos as once one of them was snatched out of the pen — no easy task because they were usually dirty and slick — the only way I could keep track was to mark them with a purple disinfectant spray. Later, we came up with a better system.

My brother got an old grocery cart from an auction or flea market and so then I'd grab up all the piglets from one mama and put them in the cart. About the only way to inject them was to hold them upside down and give it to them in one of the fleshy haunches. I learned to do this as quick — and I hoped, painlessly — as possible, but there is a reason for the expression "squealing like a stuck pig." Like human babies, the small, quick injection produced bloodcurdling screams and frantic wiggling. At times like that, I feared I'd accidentally stick myself with some swine medicine, which I think Bill would have greatly enjoyed due to his lifelong, debilitating case of "schadenfreude," or delight in the misfortune of others, especially relatives. The challenge became to draw the proper amount of medicine from a glass bottle into a syringe, hold the pig steady, get the job done, and return the baby to its infuriated mother. It was also hot in the houses, and soon I was dirty and smelling no better than the hogs. But it had to be done, and on the same day to keep the records straight and the animals healthy.

Mortality was inevitable sometimes, no matter what we did. Sometimes a piglet wouldn't eat. Sometimes they would get killed by the sow. Sometimes they would get sick. Sometimes, they just died with no explanation. These were without a doubt the worst days. Piglets, even dirty ones, are cute creatures, and finding a dead one was sad. Then, there was the financial impact of a lost animal, the gamble in all farming. Retrieving and disposing of the body was no fun, either. No matter what anyone says about a business where the animal is raised to inevitably become food, loss of life always hurt, and on more than one level.

•   •   •

Going out to eat barbecue or having a pig pickin' was a special time — it was about socializing or celebrating as well as getting one of the best meals of the year. Then there was the day or days for "killing a hog." This was a day of work, for storing up food for the coming year, providing for one's family, when not everything could be bought or was desired to be bought from a grocery store. It's how things used to be, and it was the original version of "farm to table."

We usually did this once a year, in the dead of winter. Where I come from, extremely cold days — or rooms that have been over air-conditioned — still bring on the remark from people over 40 of "it's cold enough to kill hogs." It took a cold day to protect the meat and certainly it made the work less miserable for those doing the processing.

Much has been written over the years about hog killing day. I was still pretty young the last time we did it, and they spared me many of the stages. I'm grateful for this. Usually the day started with someone having to put a .22 round in the back of a hog's head and then the animal had to be hung upside down to drain. These jobs fell to Daddy and my brothers and any other male who might have been recruited to help.

After that, organized chaos began. The skin was scalded and prepared to be made into cracklings, also known as pork skins. This is a salted delicacy for many and touted now as a low-carb snack. I've never had a taste for them.

They cut hams off to be salted and prepped for hanging in the smokehouse. This was my absolute favorite of all pork cuts. It is hard to beat a salt-cured ham, sliced and cooked in a skillet, often served with redeye gravy (grease, essentially) and biscuits and eggs. A well-cured piece can be as satisfying as a steak. It is not as simple as it sounds, as temperatures, improper preparation, and bugs can ruin a ham. My granddaddy seasoned his and then coated them with Sevin, a popular bug killer for row crops. He claimed it kept the bugs out and he was going to trim off the outside, anyway. I don't think any of us ever ate one of his hams, so maybe that was his point, to not have to share.

Tenderloin was another popular cut, set aside for later to be cut into chunks as a prime meat or to be stuffed into rolls or biscuits after being dusted in flour and fried. This is a popular meal in most mom and pop breakfast restaurants in the South where the old timers gather to tell stories and lies.

Mama and my sisters got little relief during the day. Stations were set up in the kitchen and in the storage building. They wrapped kerchiefs or knit caps on their heads for sanitation and packaged up pork chops, pork steak, and even the livers for those who would eat it (not me). There was bacon and fat back put away. Hocks were bagged for seasoning greens and vegetables. My brothers chopped barbecue that was put in containers to be frozen. The sausage grinder was brought out, the casings set up, and turns were taken grinding out long links into spirals made from a recipe written in Daddy's hand on the smokehouse wall. They were then cut and tied to be hung in the smokehouse or frozen. Pigs' feet were saved for some of our neighbors, a delicacy to them. Remnants of parts were made into souce or sause, a gelatinous dish that some love and others—like me — find disgusting. Daddy and many of his friends delighted in and enjoyed chitlins or chitterlings, which are intestines. These required a long amount of time to clean and when cooked smell just like what they used to hold when the animal was alive. I didn't know a man over 60 who didn't love them like they were caviar when I was growing up. Local restaurants would have chitlin dinners once a month and pack the place out with older men whose wives wisely stayed home, perhaps the Southern version of the old "New York Beefsteaks" Joseph Mitchell wrote about for *The New Yorker*. He knew what chitlins were, having grown up in eastern North Carolina himself.

Everyone who helped got cuts and bags to take home and the rest went into one of our freezers, usually enough to supply pork for a year, all wrapped in white butcher's paper and labeled with a magic marker.

Mama always seemed to know exactly what was out in that freezer and where to find it, even months later when she'd send me out to retrieve that night's supper.

After all the work was done, everyone was exhausted. I was mostly a gofer, running pans back and forth, dumping waste and trash, fetching drinks and paper and masking tape. Then men would slump down in the living room to talk and count up the bounty, how little had gone to waste. The women would head to the kitchen to cook vegetables to go with the fresh meat, a bounty of sausage, ribs, and tenderloin usually, the most popular cuts, as we all sat down to a big supper, a sense of accomplishment and purpose common among us, food secured and tradition preserved.

• • •

If I said or implied Shot Day or finding a dead pig was the worst day, that is incorrect. Castration Day was worse.

At a certain age, all the male pigs not destined to be boars were rounded up to have their testicles removed. Just like with cows, this is supposed to produce better tasting meat and of course keep animals docile.

I held each pig upside down with legs spread while Bill made two incisions with a sharp blade, in a flash removing the testicles. The first time I helped him, he disposed of them. The second time, he put them in a bucket. Fearing a prank or another awful job, I asked about it.

"We're saving them," he said.

"Yeah, but why?"

"Ain't you never heard of mountain oysters?"

"Uh, no. Well, maybe. What?"

"Yeah, they're hog nuts."

"That's not right."

"Yep."

Silence.

"Some guys at work wanted me to save them for 'em." He mentioned the names of some older men I'd heard him mention before. "They love 'em. Put flour on 'em and fry 'em, like oysters. Mountain oysters."

Already queasy from the work at hand, I gagged. This brought delight to my brother. I still wasn't sure I believed it, but when he was done, and after all future days of that work, the testicles ended up in old Cool Whip containers, put into his refrigerator to go the tire factory where Bill worked. I often wondered if my sister-in-law Deborah ever accidentally opened one while fixing dessert, but I never asked.

I was still not convinced my brother wasn't putting me on, so one night at supper I asked my parents. By that point, I was the only child still living at home, so it was just the three of us.

"Y'all ever heard of mountain oysters?"

Mama gave me a glance and a curled mouth and shook her head. Daddy looked up.

"You mean hog nuts? Old people call them mountain oysters," Daddy said.

"That's what Bill said, but I never know when to believe him. That's gross."

"Well, people eat 'em. I've eat 'em."

"You eat hog nuts?"

"Not if I can get something else."

• • •

When the floods came from Hurricane Floyd in 1999, hog lagoons all over the state overflowed and flooded, sending hog waste into rivers and streams and others places it shouldn't go. There was public outcry from citizens — understandable — but also from the very politicians that required the lagoons to be built. Hog farmers were blamed solely for the problem, moratoriums on growth were started, and many family farms were designated as "factory farms." A friend of mine has two employees besides his wife and kids and his operation is considered a factory. Nearly two decades later, out-of-state lawyers descended on farm communities to help bring lawsuits against farms for being a "nuisance." They put several out of business. I remember talking with an agricultural extension agent from a coastal county about one large farm operation and government interference for a magazine story I was working on. His story covered the lunacy of what farmers sometimes face.

"A stream ran through the farm and it tested for high amounts of feces," the agent told me. "The farm's cows had access to it. So they [local officials] made them fence off access to the stream. It cost thousands of dollars, plus they had to refigure how the cows would get water. Later, they found out it wasn't the cows, the stream was in the migratory path of some bird and it was bird waste."

And that's why farmers always feel like they are fighting someone or some thing to make their living — the elements, disease, people, the government.

• • •

In the third house, where the pigs stayed until they were the size and age to ship out on big trucks, they were kept in double decker cages with access to food and water and elevated off the floor. Rats would try to raid the food supply.

Sometimes my brother would wake me up in the middle of the night and we'd load our .22s with rat shot. We'd slip into the house with flashlights, flick them on and take care of the pest problem. It was amazing how many rodents he could take out before they scrambled out of holes or under doors. It was a needed task and a very country solution to a problem.

Such events were mixed, though. While it was a raw, exciting thing to do, it meant another shower. And that's where one of my biggest problems arose with working in hogs. The smell of being in the houses, the heat, the humidity, it does something to your body. The smell would get up my nose and I could never completely get rid of it. I can remember feeling like a coal miner when I'd blow my nose after working an afternoon and my tissue would look like I'd been in a coal mine. Before supper, I'd take off my boots and coveralls that I wore at the hog houses and store them in the pantry or back porch, depending on the severity of odor. I took showers and scrubbed and washed my hair and then I'd step out and could still smell it. Sometimes I'd take two showers, and I felt like I could still smell manure. If it was a weekend and I was going out with my friends, I'd have Mama sniff my hair and skin.

"I can't smell anything, you're fine," she'd say.

I'd look at my pale arms and hands, red from scrubbing and hold them to my nose. Hog shit. I used all kinds of soaps and cleaners until I was raw and chafed to no avail. I'd ask my friends if they could smell it. No. But I could.

"It's in your head," Mama said. "One way or the other."

I felt like I had enough social problems without risking a fresh-off -the-farm emission. There was always a lot of anxiety those nights. I had no one tell me I stunk, and since it was the 1980s, a brutal time to be a teen, I felt sure they would have if it had been so.

• • •

I learned a lot about the reality of farm life and the brutality of it. That time was punctuated by my dislike of anything farm related — except the good, fresh food it produced — and my desire for rebellion in some form. I'm sure my disinterest came off poorly and aggressive to the rest of my family, all of whom toiled in it much longer than I did and maybe they thought that I thought I was too good for farming. I guess in a way I did. Or at least I thought there were better ways to pay the bills and spend the length of a day. I was the first generation of my family to be expected to go to college. There were certainly many before me capable of going, but costs and expectations and life sent them in other directions.

I was straddling a time, with others in my generation, certainly many of my schoolmates, between modern and old-time ways. Between the agricultural way of life that was the only life for most in our part of the world and the coming time when farmland would become housing developments and the farms that stretched as far as the eye could see, from one town to the next, became fewer. My generation was the connector between those who were expected to labor and grow their food and food for others, and the generations that followed who chose other paths, who shopped in stores, and later, farmer's markets for their food and for whom it didn't feel strange to buy vegetables in cans, or shrink-wrapped cuts of pork and beef, food from hundreds or sometimes thousands of miles away.

My children know the joys of sleeping late in the summer and streaming movies and shows and eating takeout way too often or quick, simple, homemade meals. Life is not set up for a meat-and-three dinner table any longer, for days in the field, for evenings shelling beans or peas or shucking corn. As I thought many times in my youth, I have not missed that. I don't want to send my children to the field or spend so much time and energy on producing what we eat. I can't deny that. However, I worry that not knowing how the world works, not having to toil and sweat and suffer, to worry over the weather and the crop, that I've deprived them of something important.

I worry that having had that experience, no matter how much I disliked it or complained or muttered over it, shaped me in ways I don't realize or understand. Maybe those callouses brought character and those scars some appreciation, even if for a time and a life I don't want to return to, but perhaps just savor for a minute or two every so often.

11
Splitting Wood

By God, that man loved splitting firewood. Or more accurately, he loved his wood splitter.

On too many Saturday mornings of my teenage years, my daddy would clomp into my bedroom and smack the end of my mattress or shake my legs.

"Boy! Are you going to sleep all morning? Get up, we got wood to get."

I'd make a grumbling 80s teenager sound and look at my clock. Sometimes it was 6 or 7 a.m., depending on whether it was winter or summer. It didn't matter the time of year, the man always felt a need for stockpiling firewood.

Daddy's need had arisen, in my informed and all-knowing 13-to-18-year-old brain, because of the wood splitter he had recently purchased. It was a rusty steel I-beam with a trailer hitch on one end, and a gas-powered motor on the other. The motor powered a hydraulic arm that pushed a flat piece of steel towards a large, sharpened wedge near the trailer hitch end of the splitter. Someone held a cut piece of tree trunk, and the splitter would slice it right in half, one piece falling on either side, to be picked up again and cut into a smaller piece, and then cut again into an ever smaller piece. The someone was almost always me and the process continued until Daddy nodded the pieces were small enough for the wood stove in the living room.

That man loved his wood splitter right behind dipping bread into butter and molasses after supper and just ahead of walking around after 6 p.m. with no pants on.

Compounding this problem for me was that my brother-in-law, John, who was like a brother, got a new chainsaw. It was a really big, really loud, really powerful chainsaw and he fell hard in love with it, as my daddy had with the wood splitter. Together with this new pairing of power equipment, their relationship was never better, bonded over an insatiable appetite for hardwood. Neither could wait until the weekend to take our tractor, hitch it to an old tobacco truck, and hitch the wood splitter to a truck, pile me and my equally disgruntled nephew Bud in the back of one or the other and head into the woods on the farm to take down an unsuspecting tree or two.

Maybe that sounds like the memory of an ungrateful teenager, and maybe it is. I really just wanted to sleep, and Bud just wanted to watch cartoons. We didn't want to be sweating in the woods, watching for briars and ticks and snakes and keeping an eye on two crazed men having their Tool Time with Tim Taylor moments in the woods. They were a hazard to others and themselves. More than once I saw John cut a tree in the wrong place or almost trip while he ran that chainsaw full blast. I'd yell, and he'd act like it was all planned, grinning. I swear Daddy almost sliced my fingers and hands off on numerous occasions, getting trigger-happy flipping that lever to snap pieces of log into nice, splintery wedges of light brown, their smell crisp and sharp and lingering.

If only that was the end of it.

We cut wood in the near dark early light of winter, when it was close to or at freezing, when knit caps and long pants and socks and gloves kept the cold at bay, but we quickly built running sweat. And as they got better at running their machinery, it seemed Bud and I could do little right. We were too slow. We weren't stacking the wood right. We weren't putting the pieces on in the right order. The machines were loud, but the yelling could be louder and the language coarser as the day went on. "Dammit, Michael" was the standard.

Bud and I became co-conspirators. How could we disable the machines and make it look like an accident or an oversight? Wasn't there some club I could trick these two into joining, one that met on Saturday mornings? Could we make a case that these two insane men were going to end up clear cutting the entire farm?

When enough wood was loaded on the trailer that it looked like it might turn over, and when the bed of the truck was about to drag the ground, if every tree cut down had been split, we could get out of the woods. The loads were taken to the barn and John and Daddy would disappear inside our house to join Mama and my sister Carol as they worked on finishing supper. They tasked Bud and I with stacking the wood and then making sure an equal share went into John's truck for transport to their house in Nashville, the small town where they lived, butted right up next to Rocky Mount. We often calculated that at any one time there was enough wood to last until I retired. Both homes supplemented the heat with central air systems, so it seemed excessive.

One Saturday, Bud and I were particularly disgusted at our station in life, oppressed young men, and he let a piece of wood fly too hard and too high into the back of his dad's truck. It hit the back glass and shattered it. Bud went into a panic, because John was a spanker, and he loved that truck, just behind golf and just ahead of wearing pants in the most horrifying colors on the spectrum and now Bud's short life was coming to an end. We finished loading the wood and cleaned up the glass and went inside to deliver the news.

"Hey, um…" Bud started.

I interrupted him. "I'm really sorry John, but I threw a piece of wood on the back of the truck, and it skidded, and knocked the back glass out of your truck. Man, I'm sorry."

"Dammit, Michael," came the instant, expected response from daddy.

Bud looked at me in an admiring way I'm not sure I've ever seen from anyone else, not even many years later when I pulled a giant splinter out of my son's foot or removed an embedded tick from his brother's ear, both heroic, life-saving maneuvers to them.

"Don't worry about it, man. It's just a truck window. It's old. It was bound to happen anyway with you two dummies throwing wood around." The old part was true. When we looked down at the gas pedal, we could see the ground through the rusted out places in the floorboard.

Then we all sat down and ate steak and a baked potato and tossed salad. It was unbelievably good, and Bud seemed to enjoy his more than usual. And that was the thing, I was always bone tired and dirty, and still missing the day I could have had every time we did this, but we always finished the day with a good meal and a movie or something on those Saturday nights that involved a lot of laughing and teasing.

I helped cut wood until I was out of college. It seemed like it would go on forever, but it didn't. Both of them ended up putting in gas logs years later, not long after someone snuck into the barnyard one night and stole daddy's wood splitter. He was devastated, even though years later it was revealed that Bud and I had been prime suspects. We think they were joking.

I don't have anyone with whom to relive those memories, the good and the bad, the looking back now as opposed to the living it then. John passed away after an accident and Daddy's heart finally gave out. Bud lives on the other side of the globe. The woodstove no longer serves — it's in the old packhouse, under discarded furniture and layers of dust and abandoned wasps' nests. My sons asked what it was, and I tried to think of a clever way of saying a device for ruining Saturdays, but I couldn't.

Instead, I remembered it produced the best heat I've ever experienced, something Daddy and Mama said all the time. Not too dry, not too hot, sweet smelling. It's the heat I loved to stretch out in front on the floor in our house. I don't want to go back and cut firewood again, there is no nostalgia involved with that. But I'd love to have a steak dinner with my people and listen to them and look at them and laugh with them one more time.

12

Southern Culture on the Skids

"What the hell is hoop cheese?"

"Hey, Brantley, do you know what this is? I don't think I've ever seen that color before."

I was one aisle over in a Harris Teeter Express in Charlotte. Two of my MFA classmates, one from New York and the other from Michigan, had stumbled onto a cultural staple of my childhood. I couldn't believe they'd found hoop cheese in 1) Harris Teeter, a fairly upscale grocery store and 2) in Charlotte, a city that doesn't exude "rural" or even "southern" sometimes. (They once branded themselves as "Charlotte, USA," skipping the North Carolina part.)

"Hoop cheese? That's a delicacy, a real treat," I yelled back. It was late and there was hardly anyone in the store, a short drive from our campus. We were loud and the workers probably assumed drunk, which we were not.

Hoop cheese had been a staple on our table all my life. However, as my friends pressed me for answers — I might have been the only native North Carolinian in the MFA program, so I was the default expert/translator/redneck — I realized that while I instantly could feel the taste and smooth texture and goodness of hoop cheese on my tongue, the smoothness, the fake orangeness, I wasn't sure I could explain it. I turned the next aisle, and they were waiting, pointing to the basket, one of them turning the package over, looking for an explanation, but there was only weight and price.

"Well?" Michigan asked. She was a journalist and liked answers.

"It's good stuff," I said. "When you want to get fancy, you grate some on your grits." The first week of school, a year before, I had helped them decipher the way to eat grits, avoiding the heresy of adding sugar. "But you can put it on just about anything."

"Is it like cheddar?" New York asked. I knew she was thinking wine pairing.

"That's a weird color," one of them said. "That can't be natural."

"It's kinda like cheddar, but not really. Wine-wise, I'd go with Coke or Pepsi or sweet tea. I don't think anyone has ever drunk wine with hoop cheese. It's not really like anything, it's hoop cheese, it's its own category." It was the best I could do at midnight.

They walked away, mumbling, partially about what they needed to get before we headed back to the dorms, partially about my lack of helpfulness. I stood for a minute and remembered how we always had a block of hoop cheese in the fridge when I was a young boy. It was covered in cheesecloth and as I got older, it had a red wax rind. We always kept it in the fridge, although as I remember, it was always on a shelf or in a basket in the meat department, not usually in a cooler—sometimes in gas stations, I'd seen it under a glass cake cover and stand.

Curious, I looked up hoop cheese on the Internet and even it couldn't agree. One site called it queso blanco and said it was white. Another referred to it as a dessert cheese. The only thing agreed upon was that the cheese is made with the drained whey, which is poured into a round mold with no salt or cream added. Different websites had it as salty, rubbery, nutty, "rich yellow," spoils fast. None of those things are true.

I know that the cheese is hard to find now and very often around $7 a pound. I know it was inexpensive when I was a child and was sold in every grocery store, country store, and most gas stations — so much so that it was no more a delicacy that I'd claimed to my northern friends than a pack of Nabs.

• • •

I was an adult before I realized not everyone knew what a Nab was. The National Biscuit Company (Nabisco) cellophane-packed six sandwich crackers with peanut butter in the middle and sold them in the 1920s. At a nickel apiece, the snacks became really popular and the name NABs was adopted over "Peanut Sandwich Packet." Later on, snack company Lance Inc. started making something called Toast-Chee, which is still produced and sold in every legitimate gas station and convenience in the South. I've never heard a person called them Toast-Chee, not even the delivery people. Everyone calls them Nabs.

Nabs were often an afternoon snack for me after school. When we got back home, I'd grab a Pepsi or Mountain Dew or Orange Crush, spread the newspaper out on the table, and grab a pack of Nabs. Sometimes, I'd take them apart like people do with Oreos. Other times, I'd just crush them against the roof of my mouth, letting them dissolve with the cola, a mix of carbonation and salt that set my mouth tingling.

My daddy bought them by the case from the Lance man who delivered to the welding supply company where he worked. He also brought home crates of soft drinks in glass bottles. Sometimes, he'd bring the little bags of salted peanuts.

I'd seen him and my siblings pour their peanuts into a Pepsi bottle after taking a couple of swigs. The churning and fizzing looked like a science project. And everyone seemed to think this was one of the best things a person could do, combining snack and drink into one experience. I wanted to imitate this as I wanted do most things my brothers and sisters did, but it was on Mama's Warning List, because as a child I'd likely choke to death, which seemed certain was the destiny of my siblings, if they continued on their rebellious path of peanut-Pepsi chugging. There were many things on Mama's Warning List: don't use a garden hoe (or shovel) as a pole vault, because you might rupture yourself; don't get close to the edge of the pond, you might fall in and drown; stay away from people walking down the road, they might be serial killers or kidnappers; cross your windshield if a black cat runs in front of your car or you'll have bad luck. There were many others.

"Don't you put those peanuts in that drink," mama would say when she saw me snag a pack. "You'll choke to death and I won't be able to save you. It's happened."

Finally, one day she was hanging clothes on the line and I poured my peanuts in an ice-cold Pepsi. It crossed my mind that I might choke and die while she was outside hanging clothes on the line and that would be an awful tragedy and I hoped they'd miss me if it happened. I watched the fizz and churning and turned that bottle up anyway, letting the peanuts swish around, crunching them, feeling the salt amid the burning fizz.

In no time, the drink and the peanuts were gone, nothing left to savor, and frankly, it wasn't all that great. I don't think I ever tried it again.

• • •

There were other snacks, those that served the sweet tooth.

Little Debbie Swiss Rolls were my mama's favorite, and we always had a box of those twin little chocolate cake layers wrapped around cream and dipped in chocolate. There were especially good in the summer after being in the fridge for a day. Mickey (the baking company) made a French Pastry, which was not anything French or exotic, just a plain yellow cake with a small cream filled depression on top in the middle, also dipped in chocolate. Some people liked Twinkies and there was a time when I was seven or eight years old and begged for them every time we went in the grocery store, but that was because there were three baseball cards on the bottom of every box that could be cut out when the snacks were gone. I still have my Henry Aaron card and I marveled at how small the bat looked in his giant bear-paw hands, almost like the souvenir toy bats available at games today.

About once a week, usually on the weekend, we'd have honey buns. These are the king of southern snack foods. It's a mild oblong cinnamon roll that has been dunked in a thick white icing that came off in sheets when it was bit into. Merita made the best ones, then Mickey, and then they disappeared from shelves for a while and other companies made buns with a clear coating. These were not the same. If I remember right, a honey bun had about the same amount of fat that a normal person should have in an entire day. Mrs. Freshly's brought back the classics. Mama loved to put hers in a pie pan and heat it up in the oven for breakfast. There's a similar product called a Texas Cinnamon Roll that's not as long as a honey bun, and shaped more like a traditional cinnamon roll, just bigger.

These were the staples. Other things would come and go, like Chicken and the Biscuit crackers, canned cheese, Lance cookies, Moon Pies or Big Towns, and oatmeal pies.

• • •

Watching Mama roll out her dough was watching the artist at her canvas. She laid out a piece of material she called a baking sheet — it wasn't a towel, or not what I'd later see called a baking sheet or even cheesecloth — it was a finely woven, off white material. She dusted it with flour thousands of times over the years, took her seasoned wooden rolling pin and rolled and rolled, this direction, then that, east-west, north-south, until I'd think the dough would vanish into the weave of the sheet. She'd reach into her flour bucket, dust and carry on.

Sometimes, she'd carve it into chicken pastry. But if the sugar came out, we were headed for the big time. That meant a pie or jack.

Many southern mamas made jacks. Mama would cut out a piece of dough and roll either cooked sweet potatoes or apples into what she'd turn into an envelope. We rarely had apples, but once in a while she'd dry some or just buy the dried rings and add brown sugar and white sugar and roll them up. More often, since we always had sweet potatoes, she'd boil and mash the potatoes and add butter and brown sugar. After folding the dough over, she'd pinch the edges down and then use a fork to poke air holes on top. After she'd made three or four, into her cast-iron skillet they'd go, the Crisco already melted. The pies would sizzle on one side for just a few minutes, being turned when brown with a slight blackening where the sugar leaked out, then she'd flip and they'd sizzle again. They came out and then onto wax paper to cool. She'd make a dozen before stopping, all spread out next to her stove top to cool, and all of us took third-degree burns, unable to wait until the jacks had properly cooled before snatching one. They never lasted long enough to make it to the fridge, even though I swear there were better once they'd settled and cooled off. We all knew this, but with the smell of fried pies and the memory of the last time she made these — it only happened a couple of times a year — the getting was got while it was good.

Mama made something in that kitchen every day, outside of what she produced for her shop. She was an incredible baker, and she didn't fit that stereotype of the syrupy accented, large round white woman. She was a wisp at no more than 5'3 on a good day, wearing her immaculately clean white Reebok sneakers. When I saw her with an apron and a rolling pin, there was reason to get excited, because something good was coming. There was rarely a supper without dessert. I assumed throughout my childhood this was the way it was at everyone's house, only later finding out that other people rarely had dessert. I guess that explains my lifelong battle with weight.

"What's the point of eatin' if you ain't got nothing sweet," Mama said. She'd always laugh and add, "Don't you agree?"

We had pecan pie, coconut custard pie, coconut cream pie (with meringue), coconut cake, carrot cake, red velvet cake, caramel cake — pronounced "kermel" at our house, Mississippi mud cake, dirt cake (crushed Oreos and Cool Whip), pineapple cake, devil's food cake, swiss roll cake, chocolate pie (with meringue), and chocolate layer cake and on rare occasion pig picking cake. There is something I call Redneck Baclava, which is a cream cheese and layered crust loaded with sugar and butter that's a tad heavier than its Greek cousin, but every bit as good.

Her favorite was chocolate anything, but she had a wide range. My favorite was a cousin to the jack, the sliced sweet potato pie.

Don't confuse this with sweet potato custard pie, a delicious offering in its own right and very close to a tradition pumpkin pie, only ten times better. Mama made those too, and more often, even though I'm not sure why, because from my view and later baking experience, they weren't any less trouble.

I've only seen sliced sweet potato pie made by Mama's mama, Granny Lucy, and my sister Jane. No one else in my family or in our area ever mentioned this or took it to a covered dish or potluck dinner.

First, Mama peeled, sliced and boiled sweet potatoes, I think around two or three per pie and added a little salt. A crust was made — later in life she used store bought. Once the potatoes were done, they were scooped and layered into the crust. Butter, a little flour, and then sugar went in. Then, there was a choice to be made: lemon or spice. Mama usually made one of each — adding lemon juice and then brown sugar. The other pie got allspice in place of the lemon. Another crust went on top, sealed with holes poked with a fork.

While the pie baked, she took the leftover boiled water from the potatoes, which usually had small pieces leftover and added sugar, allspice, butter, and brown sugar. I don't use allspice when I make it, I can't get the amount right to keep the pie from having a strong taste, so I use cinnamon instead. This liquid mixture is important and is heated until it bubbles.

The pie cooked until it was brown. When a slice was served, a couple of scoops of the "juice" was poured on top and it was the best thing a person could eat. Everyone in our family loved it, and there were battles and scrums, especially as the pieces disappeared. Some people who will remain nameless even resorted to hiding the pies. We only had them a couple of times a year and that scarcity caused folks to lose their minds.

The best piece, if you were lucky enough to get it, was the last piece eaten straight out of the pie pan and took all the remaining liquid.

It was so good, that more than once I requested it as my birthday cake.

Today, because my liver transplant medications have caused Type 2 diabetes, I make a "lighter" version with a low carb crust and monk fruit instead of sugar. While it doesn't taste like Mama's, it's still my favorite.

• • •

It might be heresy to say it, but not all southern or country foods are good or "fit to eat" as Mama would say.

For example, when in a restaurant and a hot dog or hamburger is listed as "Carolina style," that means they are smothered in slaw. For someone who doesn't like his/her food to touch on a plate, this is a nightmare and having a runny cabbage-based mess on a piece of grilled meat seems like a bad idea.

Southerners also eat chitlins or chitterlings, which are hog intestines. I don't care how many times they are washed, they smell like shit when being cooked. Old men love them. There used to be regular dinners of them and some restaurants had chitlin night. I tasted them twice in the same day — the first and last time.

That might not be the worst things Southerners eat. There is something called "sause" or "souse," which is leftover pig parts made into a sort of congealed salad casserole. It sounds much better than it is. Never to waste any animal parts, southerners eat brains (often with eggs), jowls, and feet off the hog. Mama told me when she was growing up during the Depression, they ate chicken feet.

Turnip greens, mustard greens — I don't know why anyone would eat those when they have collards. There's even a weed called poke weed that's made into poke sallet — which is toxic if not prepared correctly. Seems like an unnecessary risk. I pass on rutabagas, potted meat, and anything else that is served in the shape of the can it came from.

But the list of terrible things is short.

There aren't too many households that don't have fried chicken regularly. While there are plenty of places like Popeye's and Bojangle's that take the labor out, fried chicken is deep-rooted in the South. Scottish immigrants, which stocked North Carolina heavily, deep fried chicken in fat and later enslaved Africans added more seasonings to the dish to create this classic.

Barbecue — wood cooked, whole hog chopped with a vinegar-based sauce is heavenly when done right, on a par with a ribeye. It's said that Spanish explorers noted the way the natives cooked their meats on spits and platforms with smoky fires in the West Indies. The Spanish spelling of the word was "barbacoa." Later, it was the Spanish who introduced pigs to North America, and the rest is history.

Grits were a gift that American Indians shared with settlers in the 1500s, which they called "rockahomine," later shortened to hominy. This ground corn used to be for breakfast only until some genius came up with the idea to serve them with shrimp. While usually made from white corn, there are now varieties such as blue and even different grinds, including a particularly savory one from Gullah/Geechee culture in South Carolina.

Sweet pepper relish — heavily influenced by German immigrants — can make any of the aforementioned greens palatable. In the summer, green onions, cucumbers, and tomatoes sit on many tables, drenched in vinegar, salt, and pepper, ready to dress any dinner.

Biscuits used to be a hard piece of bread that could be transported and eaten in the fields or on the march or the ship of armies and navies. Then southerners got ahold of them and with the invention of baking soda in the 1800s, they became the pillowy treat we know today. Biscuits go with anything. Then there are sweet potato biscuits made by my sister that are just plain sinful.

Food defines a place and its culture. Generations may change diets and lifestyles and certainly we are more mobile and more scattered as a people than we were a hundred or even fifty years ago. It's probably better that lard and grease and things like fatback have worked themselves out of everyday life, but are the preservatives and sodium and chemicals that replaced them any better? Even the sugar in soft drinks has changed. Preserving at least some of these foods is an important aspect of southern heritage and that stereotype hospitality that certainly begins at the table. I'm still waiting on those calls from my northern friends to send a care package of hoop cheese.

13
No Deposit, No Return

I had a pretty sophisticated lifestyle for about an hour every afternoon when I was a scholar at Bailey Elementary School.

After my mom waded through the car line in our VW van, or later in the wood-paneled Mercury station wagon, we headed home. After dropping my book bag in the hall, I gathered the Raleigh *News & Observer*, still crisply folded, and spread it out on the counter. I grabbed a pack of Nabs or a Nutty Buddy or some other Lance or Tom's snack, and then an ice-cold-in-a-glass bottle Mountain Dew or Pepsi or Orange Crush before settling onto a swiveling bar stool.

There was firewood to haul to the house, or hogs to tend to, or minor jobs to do. They would come soon enough. I was allowed the time to savor that soft drink and read the headlines, study the box scores, and enjoy the comics, school behind, chores and homework ahead, but the best part of the day at hand.

•   •   •

As time changes, so does language. In the rural South where I grew up, when someone asked, "Would you like a drink?" that meant sweet tea, maybe lemonade, but usually Pepsi or Coca-Cola depending on the household. Unlike today, it certainly was not an offer of an alcoholic beverage and even letting that thought cross the mind probably meant a future of alcoholism.

I come from a long line of tee-totalers (A person who never drinks alcohol and resents you for thinking he/she would consider it). This also makes me think of the expressions "on the wagon" (not drinking) and "off the wagon," (drinking after trying not to) which I often confuse — as I think most Americans do. Our Southern Baptist household was strictly "dry," I never saw a drop brought into my house other than from a neighbor who would have one too many Pabst Blue Ribbons or Budweisers and stagger into our house in the summer and plop down with his mostly empty can at the kitchen table only to be run out by my tiny mama, with a whole lot of "you know better"s thrown at him. However, as an adult, I have found that many Southern Baptists take that no drinking thing to mean "not around church members or do it at least one town over or at home." There's even a joke: what's the difference between a Baptist and a Methodist? A Methodist will speak to you in the liquor store [and not pretend he doesn't see you].

Like many jokes, this one is centered on a truth illustrated in my family. My sister Jane makes an amazing rum cake. Rum is a key ingredient to rum cake and therefore presents a challenge. One time, Jane was planning one of these desserts and needed to purchase rum, the only problem being Mama was in the car with her. When they pulled up in the ABC Store parking lot, Mama slumped down in the seat so no one would see her. Cutting her eyes at the rearview mirror, Mama recognized quite a few people and was thankful they didn't see her, because it might have started a scandal. I'm not sure how they would have explained their presence, but it was an ongoing concern for Mama. The two of them tell this story the exact same way, but only one of them thinks it is funny — my sister, plus the rest of the family. I like to add to the story that it takes two bottles of rum to make the cake: one for the cook while cooking and one for the cake. Mama does not like this joke and refuses to eat rum cake despite assurances that the alcohol cooks out.

While alcohol is more publicly accepted in the South and Bible Belt than it was when I was growing up 40 years ago, there are many more iconic and universally savored drinks. I'll admit I did not remain a tee-totaler as an adult. A glass of red wine with a steak or a cold beer with a spicy Mexican dish was a particularly good pairing. However, my liver disease and transplant sent me back to my roots of the traditional southern drinks of my youth.

For example, if there was a coat of arms for the South, sweet tea would have to be represented. English and American cookbooks date cold tea back to the early 1800s and with sugar added, they often referred to it as tea punch. In the South, it is implied and understood that this drink is to be served sweet and cold at all times. It is black tea that's been brewed — most often on a stove top pot — with water and enough sugar added to send a non-native straight into diabetic shock. Those born south of Maryland are genetically protected, although due to other generally accepted dietary habits of the region, will almost assuredly contract Type II diabetes.

Sweet tea is more than just a drink. It is perfect for socializing on a hot summer day, and in the time before iced coffee existed, it was the main game in town. One reason it's so popular is that it is easy and cheap to make. It's stored in big pitchers, so there really isn't a can or bottle to keep count of how much a person has had. I can't recall anyone ever saying "that tea is too sweet." When it is not sweet enough, it is simple enough to add up to a cup of sugar per glass to get things right. If a person doesn't mind being told by an elder that "that stuff will kill you faster than sugar," Sweet and Low is a fine substitute. Sweet tea is a thirst quencher and a nerve settler, but works just as well with food. It pairs with barbecue, steak, pork chops, chicken, game, and probably vegetarian meals as well, but I've yet to find a native Southerner that can confirm this.

Sweet tea is also a cultural marker. As I wrote in *Memory Cards*, if a person goes into a restaurant and the tea is not sweet when the waiter delivers it, be advised your meal is not likely to be good. The sweeter the tea, the more likely a quality meal is on the way. This can also be confirmed by the taste of complimentary hush puppies, which must be sweet or oniony; otherwise, you are in the wrong place.

Next in line is a competition like Mac v. PC, Chevy v. Ford, Republican v. Democrat, Duke v. Carolina — Coca-Cola v. Pepsi. These two soft drinks have a complicated history. A pharmacist invented Pepsi in New Bern, North Carolina, as a cure for dyspepsia (indigestion). Later, the company was sold and eventually moved to New York. Another pharmacist invented

Coke in Atlanta as a "temperance drink" and as a cure for various diseases, including morphine addiction — caffeine and cocaine were the key ingredients. The company stayed put in the city. And in some convoluted circumstance that I can only attribute to a form of communism, one can only get one soft drink or the other in most restaurants because of a complicated business situation called a "contract." Customers have been annoyed for years when ordering a Coca-Cola only to be asked if "Pepsi" was okay (or vice versa).

At any rate, both drinks are quite good in their own right. Before the early 1980s when no one was allergic to peanuts (it seemed that way, at least) many people would pour a cellophane pack of Lance or Tom's peanuts into a standard glass bottle of Coke or Pepsi. After a slightly alarming fizzy chemical reaction occurred, a distinct treat could be enjoyed and while I suppose it would be considered dangerous in today's times to drink a peanut, I recall no news items about injuries.

My grandmother Lucy used to make a very special mixed drink with Pepsi. She would add a few splashes of the drink to her sweet tea. It seemed pretty exotic at her house, but admittedly was kind of weird when consumed at home. It's no stranger than filling half a glass with iced tea and then finishing it with lemonade and calling it an Arnold Palmer.

I went through stages and I distinctly remember an addiction to Mountain Dew — invented in the 1940s as a drink mixer by a couple of Tennessee brothers. Along with regional favorite Sun Drop, it was the only "yellow drink" for a long time, until Mello Yello came along in 1979. The other attraction of Mountain Dew was the bottle. They were green with a long neck and the art on the bottle was the panel of a hillbilly with a long rifle taking a shot at a revenuer. Long before the soft drink, Mountain Dew was a term for moonshine and was even made famous by a song of the same name by Grandpa Jones. There was also another logo on the neck of the bottles at one time with the hillbilly holding a bottle and the cork flying off and putting a hole in his hat.

I never saw much in the way of moonshine. An old man down at the crossroads near my house was said to make it, and I recall as a young boy seeing the door of his outhouse blown open and a kettle inside with hoses running from it. There were frequently moonshine busts in the local newspapers, but I never saw any names of customers. I had a cousin once show me his stash in his bedroom closet. We were teenagers, but he was younger than me.

"Hey Mike, check this out." He unscrewed the cap on the jar.

"Oh my God." I was a couple of feet behind him, but the smell took my breath away, sort of a paint-thinner crossed with gasoline notion. It was as clear as water when he held it to the light.

"Want a sip?

"I'm going to take a raincheck on that. I think it almost burned a hole in my face."

My cousin laughed. "Naw, it's a lot better than what they sell in stores." He laughed some more, but decided not to take a sip either as the room started to smell like the chemistry lab at school, which brought more concerns to me later.

A few years later, my best friend tried to get me to go with him to a honky-tonk out in the country. He was an adventurous type and had heard many stories about the joint, which sounded exactly like the plot of the Porky's movies. There was even a big bad owner who legend claimed cared about cash, not IDs. I could only imagine what the crowd would be like and what reactions they'd have to two obvious teenagers strolling in.

"Every way I look at this, we end up calling our parents. From the hospital, from the jail, from a phone booth after crawling down the road with knives stuck in us," I said.

"You're crazy man. No one would leave their knife in us."

"I think you're missing what I'm saying."

"Don't be a wuss."

"I don't know, man. I don't think wanting to avoid getting my ass kicked for no reason makes me a wuss."

"You worry too much."

"Yeah."

My buddy took pity on me and we did something else totally worthless. A couple of weeks later, he went without me. But he never would tell me anything about it. I just know he never went back after that.

• • •

Almost extinct are the "ades" — lemonade, orangeade, and limeade. Most people make lemonade from a powder that comes in a can and then just slice a few lemons to float on top of the pitcher. Lemonade was one of those things that could make a person thirstier after consumption. But an Orangeade wasn't something that could be duplicated. The fruit was sliced, put into a press and squeezed into a glass with ice and simple syrup or lots of sugar added, with some ice. There was nothing else like it and many drug store soda counters offered them, but they are rare now, sometimes appearing at farmer's markets and fairs.

• • •

Once upon a time, my friends and I thought Gatorade was the greatest drink in the world. After seeing athletes drink it during games, it became available on grocery shelves in powder form only. I remember talking mama into buying me a can in Bass Brothers, the local general store, one summer day when it was sold with a free sports bottle — it looked just like the one pro football players were using. I guess it was about 16 ounces, green plastic with white and orange lettering and the old Gatorade logo with a lightning bolt. No matter what I did, I could never keep it from being gritty — too much powder settled to the bottom, not enough made it watery. I remember when it started being offered in the pre-made form and sold in glass bottles that people were skeptical folks would pay a premium to just have the water already added — this was of course in the pre-bottled water days. There was no recycling of the bottles.

It really was refreshing during a game and I can only imagine the benefits it would have had for my family and those who helped us in the fields when I was a child. Later, I remember doctors recommending it to help during sickness and I have to say when I'm under the weather, a Gatorade or Ginger Ale is all I want.

There are still some mixes today, but when I tell my children about how it was only available in powder, they give me the look of an ancient.

•   •   •

I never thought about ginger ale being a mixer when I was a kid. I developed a taste for it in the early 1970s as a preschooler. I had a brother and sister each have weddings when I was six and ginger ale was the primary ingredient, along with pineapple juice and some other weird things that produced unnatural colors for the punch bowl. My sisters would always save me a little ginger ale at the showers and receptions I was dragged to, and I always appreciated the bubbles and the soothing fizz on my throat. The only brand I ever saw was Canada Dry, which had real ginger, not that I really knew what that was other than an important sounding claim on the label. I only remember seeing it in 64 ounce bottles, the forerunner to two liters.

•   •   •

There is an old southern stereotype of a RC Cola and a Moon Pie as a classic southern snack combination. RC is a little less distinctive tasting than a Coke or Pepsi, so maybe that is why. It was a drink developed out of spite by a grocer who became bitter that he couldn't get a discount on the large quantities of Coca-Cola syrup he was buying and vowed to make his own drink. A Moon Pie is a soft chocolate-covered graham cracker cookie sandwich with marshmallow in the middle, produced in Tennessee. It originated based on the inventor asking a coal miner what an ideal snack would be. It was filling but light and was popular among the people who barned tobacco with us as a mid-morning snack — that or the Lance version called a Big Town, which is no longer produced.

Another popular drink was Orange Crush, an extremely sweet, caffeine-free orange soft drink. My wife became addicted to these drinks when she was pregnant and had to back off caffeine. Crush also made a chocolate drink that was like a Yoo-Hoo and a grape drink. Crush got a competitor when Sunkist debuted in 1979. Sunkist seemed more carbonated, but I mostly remember the brilliant marketing plan of "Good Vibrations," the Beach Boys song, used in all the ads. That same year, Mello Yello (Coca Cola) debuted as a competitor for Mountain Dew (Pepsi). It was a hit, and I had a cousin who was obsessed with it. Dr. Pepper was also quite popular, and the summer I worked for Coca-Cola it became my drink of choice. I also found what looked like an old coffee maker at the Coca-Cola plant in Rocky Mount one day, and it was supposed to be used to serve Dr. Pepper warm, as an alternative to coffee. The old bottles used to have the numbers 10, 2, 4 as the recommended times to drink one to pep up. Coke now has Mr. Pibb Xtra, a reformulation of Mr. Pibb, which debuted in 1972. It was remade with a little cinnamon in 2001 — hence the Xtra.

A wild card in all this was another North Carolina drink that was strictly regional until the last few years, Cheerwine. It's a highly carbonated drink that's cherry flavored, along with lines of Dr. Pepper or Mr. Pibb, but more sweet than zingy.

Those were our drinks.

And they were all treats, set aside for a particular time of the day: after school, after supper, during a break from hard, hot labor. We paired them with things like Nabs, Nutty Buddies, Oatmeal Pies, Raisin Cakes, Moon Pies, honey buns, Little Debbies (later immortalized in the Southern Culture on the Skids song, "Camel Walk"), Twinkies or salted peanuts. It was a boost to get a person to the next meal.

· · ·

The kind old lady who lived next to my grandparents in the 1970s was a loyal 7Up drinker. I'd often visit her when we made the short ride, because she was kind and had a house packed with all kinds of plants and flowers.

7Up contained a mood-stabilizing drug until the late 1940s and was originally called Bib-Label Lithiated Lemon-Lime Soda and launched just weeks before the stock market crash of 1929 kicked off the Great Depression.

Mrs. Whitley never failed to offer me a bottle or at least half of one. Those bottles were tapered with a long neck and had the white lettering and red dot. But we never drank out of the bottle at her house. She'd have me climb up in a kitchen chair as she dropped ice cubes into her ice crusher, a device that looked like a cross between a small transparent cooler and a mixer. We'd loudly grind enough ice for two glasses. It was cold and clear and I could feel the bubbles in my nose as we made our way to the living room, me asking her to name all the flowers she was growing and she answering as we climbed into the seats in front of her black-and-white TV to watch "Jeopardy" or reruns of "Sanford & Son."

• • •

I think the strangest thing in drinks in my lifetime has been bottled water. The only bottled water I knew of was Perrier, and it was fizzy and weird and seemed like something used only in movies or by rich people to make cocktails. Out in the country, we drank unfiltered water from the tap, straight from our well or better yet, from the water hose in the yard. It was not great for taking that dusty taste out of one's mouth and the water out of taps from my friends who lived in town was undrinkable. We didn't know until marketers got together and told us all that was bad for us, that only water packaged in plastic bottles was fit for consumption. It may or may not be boiled first. I think my grandparents would have thought we'd lost our minds if they saw us not only paying for water, but sometimes paying more than what soft drinks or beer cost. The only thing I think of comparable is the marketing of "Black Angus" beef, which implies that the color of a cow's hide affects flavor or quality.

• • •

Most of the soft drinks I consume today have a Zero as part of the name — variations of Mountain Dew, Sprite, Coca-Cola and others — meaning there is no sugar. While they taste better than the original diet drinks, there is admittedly some question about the long-term health effects of the substitute — the "zero" ingredient. Tea has to be ordered unsweetened — which almost always gets me a funny look from the waitress until I ask for Sweet n' Low on the side. Things change.

• • •

We'd ordered Mexican food from our favorite local place, El Paso Restaurant in Bailey. When my son and I returned with the orders, I fixed my usual RTIC cup of ice water, but I also popped the top on a tall glass bottle of Coca-Cola that had been in the fridge for about a week.

I'm not supposed to have a "real" Coke because my transplant meds have given me Type II diabetes. I usually stick with water and coffees or diet drinks, but on this night, I've decided to splurge. My burrito is delicious as always, but the Coke heightened the balance of sweetness and carbonation, in the same way that beer pairs especially well with spicy food.

There are a couple of reasons why this Coke is particularly good. One, is because it is in a glass bottle and for reasons I can't explain, that makes a difference. The Coke was sold from the shelf as "from Mexico," an odd distinction until you compare ingredients. Cokes made in Mexico are made with real sugar, like they were in my youth. Cokes made in the United States are made with high fructose corn syrup, a cheap and much maligned replacement. It's funny that sugary drinks brought on the diet drink craze and then a substitute came out for sugar that might be even worse. Of course, diet drinks are supposed to be harmful in their own way as well. At any rate, imported soft drinks in glass bottles carry a premium because for Gen Xers like myself and those generations before, a Coca-Cola of this type becomes not just a soda, but a time machine to a sweeter and smoother and simpler era.

There was a time when glass bottles were the only way to buy a soft drink unless it was from a fountain. Bottles were saved and replaced in the crate until the empties made up a full load and Daddy could take them back to work for when the Coke or Pepsi man made his rounds. He bought them by the crate off the truck, but in those days, the companies also made home deliveries in town. Coca-Cola eventually phased the practice out, but still had accounts that were grandfathered in, and I remember there were still a few in Rocky Mount in the summer of 1990 when I worked there.

Despite our high-tech stainless steel insulated cups, nothing holds a soft drink like a thick glass bottle. Fridges are great, but sticking the bottles in a cooler full of ice is even better — there are some barbecue restaurants that know and serve them this way.

It was rare to see drink bottles thrown out by the side of the road and even when there were, many folks walked the roadside and collected them to get the deposit from the local store — recycling was easy and convenient, an idea that has been lost to time and perhaps laziness or simply disregard for the environment as empty plastic bottles can be found in ditches, parking lots, and overflowing trashcans everywhere. There is little recycling now as it is not easy or profitable.

Glass bottles have made somewhat of a comeback, but they often carry a stamp of Non-Returnable, and then the exception states listed by abbreviation. No Deposit, No Return was the label that started appearing when I was younger and companies moved to cans and then plastic bottles.

Maybe soft drinks aren't better with sugar and maybe the container doesn't matter. Maybe it's simply my mind and a refreshing memory telling me so.

14

Southern Snow Days

It was no slo-mo movie scene where I spun in the air and hovered above the snow and ice, life flashing before my eyes, before slamming face first into the ground. It was the opposite: in a split second, I elevated, flipped, and flopped.

The crash wasn't totally unexpected. After all, I'd climbed into a flat top fiberglass kayak which was secured by rope to a 4x4 truck belonging to one of my nephews. The driver was his girlfriend, whose objective was to see how long it would take to dump me pulling the contraption over a harvested soybean field.

A niece snapped a photograph at the precise moment I went airborne and despite my significant size I look rather graceful, suspended a couple of feet in the air, spread-eagled, turned face down.

I was bundled tightly in a toboggan (known in other parts of the country as a knit cap), a canvas Land's End jacket, long johns, sweatpants, and heavy padded gloves. The damage was mostly to my pride and even before I stopped rolling, I could hear the screams of laughter from those in the back of the truck, some who had already had a turn, others who waited.

It was a southern snow day, redneck style.

• • •

The average temperature in eastern North Carolina is around 72 degrees. That sounds pretty "temperate" or "mild." It's a pretty worthless stat, really.

Summers are hotter than a Hot Pocket microwaved for five minutes, with constant humidity. Winters can be bitterly cold, with snow, ice, and sharp winds. It's also said the average snowfall is about an inch, which means snow happens too often to be rare, but it's usually not enough to be fun... only a nuisance. Travel becomes hazardous and the stores see a run on bread and milk. In rural areas such as mine — eastern North Carolina — the power often goes out, sometimes for days at a time. Everyone is locked down.

That leaves books and TV and music — when the power stayed on — and days off from school or work. Non-natives mock the lack of preparedness by locals. They don't understand why we don't have fleets of snowplows and salt trucks. Why would the DOT make such an expenditure for less than five snow days a year, and only enough accumulation every few years to matter?

For rednecks — and everyone native to eastern North Carolina has a touch of the blood that runs from a long line of "a very mutinous people" — it's a time to get out and cut loose. That means thinking creatively.

For a couple of days one winter, we got pretty creative.

• • •

There was a precedent for the snow kayaking. Back in 1980, when I was a child, we had the "Snowstorm of the Century." In early March, the eastern part of the state got roughly 18-22 inches of snow, with some places getting up to 30. Drifts were recorded as high as eight feet. There were strong, high winds, and it was extremely cold and more than a dozen people died.

We were snowed in at a time when there was nothing to stream except books and the six or sometimes seven channels we got if you included UHF. Family lived close by on what was part of my parents' farm and so our house was a central gathering place for at least part of the day. Just before the storm, we had moved an old broken recliner to the porch for its eventual ride to the dump.

My brother Bill and my brother-in-law Eddie were in the living room talking when the light bulb went off. My brother, about 20 at the time, was out the door and headed for the barn. Eddie, a few years older, started wrestling the old green-and-plaid chair through the screen door and down the concrete steps. The leg rest was locked into place, which was part of the reason it was being discarded and within just a few minutes, chains were secured around the Barcalounger's wooden runners and to the back of Bill's truck. Off they went, Bill driving and Eddie fully reclined, sliding down the road. When they got to the curve in the road, they switched places. I grabbed my little Kodak Instamatic and recorded what would become classic redneck Americana art but at the time was just another episode in the show of what my family is capable of when they are bored.

I anxiously awaited my turn as the chair slid from the edge of one ditch to the other, the chain alternating between slack and taut, the howls of laughter echoing in the cold. But it was not to be. My mama had observed the nonsense from a window, quarreling and checking off her usual list of the potential maiming or horrific deaths that would surely result. Daddy peeked through the blinds and gave his expected commentary: "Dumbasses. Two dumbasses." I think he wanted to ride as well, deep down. Bill and Eddie stopped, and I thought sure we could break Mama, but she was having none of it, again giving a list of the hazards and adding "Ain't y'all got no sense at all?"

I went in the house, disappointed as the pair made several more runs up and down the straightaway in front of our house. When they finally came inside, the old recliner was nowhere to be seen. I don't know what happened to it, and they never would tell, although I suspect at some point they sent it sailing into a ditch or field, splintering the chair in a tangle of springs and fabric and wood, still too much fun to admit Mama might be a little right, just not right enough.

• • •

One highlight wished for was to get enough snow to make snow cream. This was a very exotic treat. The snow had to be soft, not icy, and had to gathered from a clean area that was dirt free and had not yet been contaminated by animals, wild or domestic. This usually meant gathering it from a car's hood, roof or windshield.

Snow was dumped into the biggest bowl available where sugar and usually evaporated milk — although regular milk would do — were added and stirred together. It had to be eaten quickly and didn't keep and it was so good to me as a child, a hint of homemade ice cream or a milkshake. Control had to be maintained as eating it too fast was sure to cause a headache or too much a bellyache, two things that could keep a person inside and out of the snow. It was a risk we were all willing to take.

• • •

As I grew older, my love of snow days never waned.

One weatherman from a Raleigh TV station loved it as much as any kid and his excitement would always show as a storm approached. He could barely contain himself when an accumulation was in the forecast.

There is just something hard to describe about an unexpected day off, a day when obligations have to be postponed, when jobs and school work just have to wait. As an adult, letting those responsibilities fall away, even for just 24 hours, brings back the youthful release of being a child again.

As my nephews got older, a few phone calls would get us in the road playing hockey and one year after I'd taken up ice hockey there was enough for me to put my ice skates on. I quickly appreciated the work of a Zamboni as it did a number on my blades, but we all enjoyed the ridiculousness of the moment, a snapshot made for social media before it existed.

There were serious snow forts built and snowball fights. After one particularly brutal fight, a photo was taken by someone — maybe my wife — of a snowball execution of my niece, who had taken advantage of the chaos and landed head shots on all the participants in a series of changing alliances and betrayals before she was finally cornered. Redneck justice can be brutal, even in a snowstorm.

• • •

Living in the country can be a real pain in the neck sometimes.

We aren't really that far from nearby towns, just enough to make it inconvenient to have to go out after a long day. No one delivers food out our way. The internet service is slow. It is not as bad as it used to be, but we lose power often during storms, sometimes from car accidents, and sometimes when a too-tall truck comes through and pulls the ancient lines down. We used to joke that if a squirrel broke wind, the power would be out for two days.

We have to make sure we are prepared when a storm is predicted, because our road is one of the last in the county to get cleared. There is the risk of being too prepared, because food can be lost if the power stays off long.

However, perhaps the beauty of living in the country is never more apparent that just after a nice hard snow. There is a quiet and a peace that falls over the land, especially in that window of time just before sunset until dark just puts down its roots.

Sometimes my wife and I and the kids walk through the woods, across our property and that of my parents and siblings, none of us caring about boundaries. Although I've lived on this property almost all of my life, it is different, surprising, after a snow.

The air is clean and it can be seen just in front of faces. Sound carries. No traffic enhances the stillness, broken only when a bird or two that believed in the "mild winters" written about North Carolina flits from tree to tree looking dinner, which my wife happily provides in her feeders. The fading sunlight offers oranges and purples and blacks and whites across the sky. The cold promotes alertness and reminds that being outside in this is temporary. Faces tingle as do lungs as the air braces, a uniform white blanket uniting trees and road and ditches and fields and yards, no boundaries, just a clean page.

• • •

Bill's son, my nephew William, called me to let me know what I was missing. His dad was working but my sister's kids are home. By the time I arrive, they have made enough runs across the fields that there are tracks and evidence of wipeouts. Everyone is cold but smiling or laughing and recounting who has thrown whom.

"It's your turn, Mike," William announced, with clear intent that my ride won't be a smooth one, although he added, "I'll drive slow." I knew he was lying because he has too much of his dad in him and he could barely contain his smile. He knows I know. This was a setup from the beginning.

After enough protest to give my family a victory that they've somehow tricked me, I climbed onto the yellow kayak tied behind the bright red Toyota. Folks crawled into the truck bed snickering and cameras and cellphones ready to record the carnage. I thought about the recliner going down the road three decades before, how I never got my ride. I sat down, grabbed the handles on the boat, and questioned my judgment as the truck lurches into gear.

I'm skidding over rows, hills, meadow strips, all covered with inches of snow. The sun is out. Everyone is laughing. There's a sharp turn near a drift close to the end of the track. I feel the kayak separate and disappear out from under me and I'm in the air, flipping, and then crashing. I'm too old to be doing this, I think, but only for a moment.

The truck stops as I get to my hands and knees to the sounds of children laughing hard. William works to maintain a straight face. "You alright, man?" he asked.

"That was awesome," I said. And I meant it.

15
Margie's Bake Shop

From just before Thanksgiving until the week after Christmas, the smell of baking bread often reached out into the front yard. But it wasn't the smell of a mother making a special holiday dinner for her family. This was the aroma of bread baked for a purpose, in volume, bread to be sent out into the world — stores, restaurants, cafes, homes, parties.

The strains of yeast and flour, notes of sour and sweet, could not be contained by the metal doors or the bricks. The aroma entangled every visitor that entered the house, leading them down the dark hallway and into a left turn to the "home kitchen" where work usually spilled over, or sometimes straight back to the "commercial kitchen," where rows of upside-down sourdough rolls, slight, honey-brown pan marks on the bottom attesting to perfect doneness, cooled to await bagging. In the oven were always more pans, loaves and rolls. Sometimes a conflicting sweeter smell might tease sugary cinnamon rolls or blueberry loaves rising, bursting with sugar and fruit, paralyzing to the innocent visitor.

Laid out on every counter were small buckets, former family-sized ice cream containers, filled with flour and sugar and salt. Flat pans of rising dough covered in wax paper were all over, while empties were stacked near the double sink, toasted parchment papers still intact, awaiting another turn in the cycle. Each square inch was staged, and conducting in the middle of it all was a 5'2 bundle of energy, brown-permed, glasses wearing little lady whose hands seemed to emerge from dough, pinching perfect sized globs or dumping lumps into individual tins or rolling out layers or filling cake pans or stirring icing — everything at once, everything at just the right time, a symphony of work and coordination that anyone not versed in cooking might appreciate, but be lost in how to duplicate. In a movie, there would be flour on the little lady's face and perhaps on surfaces, and maybe a dusting in the air. But not here, no, that would not do for my mama's sensibilities or sanitation values.

"Grab you one of those rolls if you want one," were the words I knew were coming, because even if I didn't want one when I came in the door, I most certainly did before she could even tell me "hey." The routine was set. "They are so good when they are right out of the oven. Umm-uh. Sit down and tell me the news."

· · ·

Long before my mama started her bake shop, she was known for two things: her abilities in the kitchen and her work ethic. The woman was always moving, always doing something, and there was never a moment during a day when I was growing up that there wasn't something good, always homemade, to eat in that house, whether it was 6 a.m. or 10 p.m. And mama certainly believed the parts in the Bible about idle hands — she had that sin covered, just like her mama before her. There was no idle time until she crawled into the bed to be up at first light the next day to do it all again.

Breakfast was cooked, lunch was usually hot, and supper was at a bare minimum a meat-and-three, with dessert, every single night. My daddy expected it, I looked forward to it, and so did my brothers and sisters, even after they got married and moved out. If it sounds terribly tedious and oppressive, it was not. It was my mama at her happiest, doing what she loved — baking, frying, pickling, souping, jellying, or anything else that involved taking simple ingredients and turning them into something magnificent. She took pride in her work, habits formed in the last days of the Depression. She enjoyed pleasing people, especially her family, and her culinary fame spread. She's told my daughter more times than I can count that when she was a child and people asked her what she wanted to be, she'd always say "a mommy."

What I saw as hard, grueling work, was her in her element. I still joke that my mama enjoyed working and her hobbies included working, and her in spare time, she liked to work. In most of our lifestyles now, that doesn't seem like fun. But as I see my mama now approaching 90, widowed, slowed by arthritis, and with a cranky back and neck, she has no peace in sitting around the house unable to do. She's never been much of a TV watcher and vision loss has curbed her voracious reading, the closest thing she did to relaxing. She can't physically work anymore and it drives her crazy. I miss the fruits and carbs of her labor, but I miss her being able to create in the kitchen. It would be like a painter who can no longer hold the brush, the fiddler who can't reach the notes, the writer who can no longer find the words.

• • •

My favorite uncle, Van, mama's baby brother, shared a lot of her characteristics. A bookkeeper by trade, he had a good job, but still worked on the side doing the books for several small businesses in Rocky Mount and Nashville, the county seat. Two of his clients were country cooking grills that were open for breakfast and lunch, and the owners were looking to add a dessert menu to go with the hot dogs and hamburgers they served to workers from Rocky Mount's large manufacturing community in the late 1970s.

My parents had given up tobacco farming, and my daddy had taken an office job a half hour away in Rocky Mount. Mama worked briefly in the local high school cafeteria as a cashier, but she was wasting time and energy in such a confined position.

One day Van had a business proposition for Mama.

"Why don't you try chocolate, coconut, lemon, and sweet potato to start," Van suggested. "There's one thing... you have to slice the pie and wrap each piece individually. They're selling by the slice, they want it to be ready for the customer when they get it."

Mama balked at this as it seemed like quite a bit of extra work. But, it also presented an opportunity. I think I was in about third grade.

"I'm going to need your help, Michael," Mama said. This was my first real chance to help bring some money into our household — far from rich, but also far from the many impoverished residents in rural eastern North Carolina. We didn't have a lot of luxuries, but we had clothes, shoes, food, transportation, TV, and indoor plumbing, things not to be taken for granted even in the early 1980s.

Pretty soon, C&L Takeout and Westry's were sending dozens of slices of pie out the door each day for lunch. An inspector told the owners that since the pies weren't made in-house, they had to have labels and the name of the bakery that produced it. In a hurry, Margie's Bake Shop was named. My sister Jane used an old Royal typewriter to make a set of peel-and-stick Avery labels with the ingredients and our address. Later, she photocopied sheets for each product line. My job was to wrap slices in cellophane as Mama sliced them into perfectly apportioned wedges, and we put them back into the pie pan Trivial Pursuit style.

It wasn't long before delivery demands were too much for my uncle, so my daddy had to make deliveries. The job outgrew him as well.

Pretty soon, mama bought one of the first mini-vans, and got one where the middle seat could be removed. This became another one of my jobs, removing the seat the night before deliveries went out as that van would be filled three times a week from front to back. As word spread about her creations, some local grocery stores became interested.

• • •

"I'm going to make you rich and famous," Bobby Mears told my mama.

"How about we skip the famous part and just go with rich?" Mama replied.

Mr. Mears let out a belly laugh. He owned a tiny, but renowned grocery store on Sunset Avenue in Rocky Mount called Englewood Supermarket. The customer base was a lot of the affluent citizenry and was best known for its meat department. This opened up a new clientele for Mama. Mr. Mears was a loveable, kind, gregarious personality, and his customers often hugged him when they came in to shop. They were fiercely loyal and his endorsement and placement was big. So were his ideas.

"Cakes," he said one day. "Can you bring me cakes?" That was like asking Van Gogh if he could paint a streetscape.

"I'll bring you anything you want that you think you can sell," Mama said with a laugh. She and Mr. Mears had become fast friends, not just because he had made her little business a full-time job, but because he acted like they were partners.

"Here's what I need you to do," Mr. Mears said, "I need you to cut them in half and put them on some kind of board and wrap them. Half cakes. That's what I need."

"That doesn't seem like a good idea," Mama said. "I make whole cakes. Who would want half a cake?"

"Oh, Margie, you've got to trust me on this one. People will buy half a cake. First, they don't think they can eat a whole one before it goes bad. Then, if they buy a half, they won't feel guilty if they end up eating the whole thing themselves. And, a half will be cheaper, and no matter how much money they have, they will like that lower price."

Mama was skeptical. I knew she did not want to do it, and it seemed a little crazy. No one in my family had been anywhere and seen half a cake for sale. And I'm not sure anyone else could have talked her into it besides Mr. Mears.

He was more than right. Coconut, chocolate, caramel, Devil's Food, and double chocolate, soft and sweet and light with lots of icing, flew off the shelves and onto some of the best set tables in Rocky Mount. Mama had turned into a full-blown entrepreneur, right off the farm, a woman navigating a business in an area almost exclusively dominated by men.

• • •

Sourdough is the fermentation of dough with lactobacilli and yeast. It keeps better because of the lactic acid. Sourdough has origins in Switzerland and the Fertile Crescent, and was brought to Northern California by French bakers during the gold rush. It requires a "starter" that has to be fed every 24 hours. It is worth the trouble.

• • •

Many people in North Carolina have moonshine in their family DNA. We had a different type of fermented culture in our family. Instead of being hidden in a shed in the woods, cloudy Mason jars half full of liquid and instant potato flakes stocked an extra refrigerator in the pantry.

No one remembers exactly when sourdough came into the picture — one night a neighbor brought a loaf of bread to share. It was delicious, and she told how easy it was to make, that you needed a "starter" and then you had to "feed it" every 24 hours. Mama, who had been making cornbread and biscuits all her life, laughed and said okay. I didn't think we would remember it in a week.

But Mama tried it. The first batch was great, and the second was even better. Then she got the idea that instead of making loaves, she might try pinching the dough off and making rolls. She had a tiger by the tail.

It wasn't long before sourdough loaves were on the shelves at Englewood Supermarket, and Smith's Red and White, a store in the Dortches community just outside Rocky Mount, as well as at West Nash Supermarket in Wilson, 20 miles south on U.S. Highway 301. Those rolls were unlike anything on the shelves, and people soon learned delivery dates, knowing what we knew — that those rolls were melt-in-the-mouth, no butter or jelly or jam necessary when they were warm. (Although it is worth noting that homemade pear preserves made the best filling.) Plenty of times mama made her delivery runs while the bread was still carrying the warmth from her ovens. Sourdough became the number one seller and soon Margie's Bake Shop added shelf space in Lowe's Foods and Food Lion, two regional grocery chains.

Demand peaked at holidays, and the stretch from Thanksgiving to New Year's Day meant impossible hours considering she was still using three home ovens and no professional equipment. Maybe that is why everything tasted so good. She was using a large wholesaler for ingredients, and it was an odd sight seeing 18-wheelers back up to our storage building in the country to offload pallets of flour and sugar and other necessities.

By this time, I was in college. When mama would finally give out around 10, after working 16 or so hours, I'd take over the kitchens, cranking out rolls and loaves, trying to be as particular and consistent as she was. The ovens ran all the time. I loved staying up and watching late night TV and allowing the blanket of sweet and sour baking bread to enfold me, to surround and wrap itself around that warm kitchen as winter and the holidays descended.

•   •   •

There was another smell created, and it was the other type of bread: money. When Mama first started, what she made helped pay the light bill and other expenses. Later, when the family hog business tanked, it helped save the farm. In better times it funded Christmas presents and vacations, and gas money, and it helped pay my college tuition. Even though mama never got rich and famous, having her own earned money gave her an independence and confidence she'd never had. She grew her business to the point that when health issues and PTSD from Korea forced my daddy into an early retirement, she was the primary breadwinner, so to speak.

•   •   •

Deliveries were interesting, and I enjoyed seeing the business end of things, the excited customers, and the pleasant exchanges with store workers. It wasn't all smooth sailing and collecting payments. Margie's Bake Shop had plenty of challenges. It wasn't long into her start up when the health inspectors started showing up. Mama was an immaculate housekeeper, but as an avowed pessimist, she expected the worst. It could have been a problem if she hadn't had the foresight during an early 1980 home remodel to keep her old kitchen intact.

To have a home food business a separate kitchen had to be maintained, including stove, sink, and refrigerator. Since she had her sewing machine in the same area, and used some of the cabinet space for storage, all that had to be moved to other rooms. Certain inspectors were prone to finding obscure violations unless lots of samples were made available to take home for "further inspection" (is that a spool of thread? Well, I could shut you down for that), essentially small-scale extortion.

She also had one store in whose owner was a gracious and helpful man and who was hoping his two children would be able to take over the business. They had a rivalry and attitudes that indicated a less than bright future. The son suffered from some sort of small man's disease-meets-son-of-successful-well-liked-man disorder. He loved to make vendors wait to be checked in, even when he had nothing to do and the store was practically empty, just to make sure everyone knew who was in charge. One day, I finally sought some relief.

"Hey Jack*[2], what time would be best for me to deliver in the morning so I can get to class on time and maybe make it easier for you?"

"It's already easy for me. I don't care when you come, you're going to wait." I held my tongue, and he gave me that smug smile before turning and walking away.

His next thing was to slap the items when he counted them. No one else we delivered to did this. And why would they? Mama spent a lot of time making sure every item looked great under the clear cellophane wrapper, and we made sure the label was visible but out of the way. Jack started slapping harder and harder, leaving dents and holes in the product. Items that didn't sell had to be picked up and credited to the store, a lost sale that couldn't be recovered. This upset mama terribly, and finally one day, I'd had enough.

"Can you be a little gentle when you count? You're making gashes in the cakes."

"I'll count however I damn please and if you don't like it, you can quit bringing your cakes."

"Now why would you want to me to do that? Everybody makes money when everything sales out. If it's damaged, people won't buy it. You know

---

[2] Not his real name

that." I stepped closer to let him know I wasn't intimidated. I was a good six inches taller, plenty arrogant, and testosterone heavy at 21 — and this was my mama he was messing with.

"Don't be a smartass with me."

"It's fine," I said, surprising myself. "I'll take it up with the boss. We both know what he's going to say." I went into the office and mentioned the problem. The dad liked money a lot. The cake slapping stopped, but the tension never did.

• • •

Eventually, breads and cakes far surpassed pies in sales and certainly in profit margin. Whole pies had to be put in nice, but expensive boxes and did not have a long shelf life. Chocolate, lemon, coconut custard, coconut cream, pecan, and sweet potato pies became special order only. Cakes sold well, but the specialty breads were like no other item. There was a blueberry sourdough loaf that was topped with a powdered sugar-based icing that was like a cross between a doughnut and a honey bun, packed with fresh local berries. Cinnamon rolls always sold out. Forget the national icons, these were decadent, soft, airy rolls packed with brown sugar and cinnamon and topped with that same glaze. I can only liken them to a Krispy Kreme donut in their uniqueness. Banana loaves and sweet potato rolls weren't iced, but were popular items. Mama even briefly bottled my dad's vinegar-based barbecue sauce and her homemade French dressing, but the bottles and process were time-consuming and didn't have the margin or volume of the baked goods. She figured out a way to salvage leftover loaves and rolls — she cut, seasoned, and baked them into short runs of croutons. They always sold out.

For over 20 years, Mama ran the bake shop like a well-oiled machine. It got to be more work than she could handle solo. She did not charge "boutique" prices one might get in today's economy for special, handmade delicacies, and she didn't make enough to support good help. Several stores were making changes as more chains moved to the area. I needed additional help at the studio, and I told mama when she tired of the baking, she had a job. I didn't think she'd be able to give it up, but when she found out my wife and I were expecting our first child, she saw a good ending point.

It was sad but a good move. Mr. Mears passed away and his property was sold and a chain drug store stands there now. The "little man's" store was sold to make way for another chain drug store. Smith's opened its own deli. Neither of those takeout restaurants she started with is open, both having been demolished after closing.

• • •

I never turned down a sourdough roll or a cinnamon roll or blueberry bread at Mama's house, as my waistline will attest. I could not think of much news to share when eating those treats, only about getting lost in the sugar rush. Like so many things that become memories, I never thought I'd not have those things, never thought my mama wouldn't be running her kitchen like a tiny, possessed dynamo. But, there is no longer starter in Fridge #4, and I don't know the last time I tasted sourdough. We used to talk about making starter or having a big bread-making day, but it never happened — she's feeble now and her kitchen days are over. My children barely remember the bread and cinnamon rolls. I should step up and do something about that. I fantasize every once in a while about bringing the bake shop back to life, but then remember the work and the risk and wonder if people care about homemade, or even if the word carries the meaning and power that it once did. It makes me admire and appreciate Mama's courage and savvy even more.

Margie's Bake Shop is where I found my love of cooking, not just the items for sale, but the meals I learned to make so Mama wouldn't have to. I had a role model, a strong woman, to show me how to run a business and a kitchen—make all you can while opportunity is there, but only if you can make a quality product. "Eat the imperfections and learn" applies to more than bread and cakes.

People who came over to my parents' house were always looking something to eat, and they usually found it, whether they were family or salesmen or friends or the preacher. It was work and love and prosperity, all at once earned and spent and enjoyed. The walls of that house haven't given up the past easily, and sometimes, usually in the change of seasons, I get a whiff of that sourdough and I'm hungry all over again.

16
Muddy Waters: Roll on Tar River

There's a dirt mound to climb over and briars and weeds that seem to grab at ankles. In the summer, there might be snakes. Once that's been conquered, the ghost bridge offers a view unlike any in the county.

The concrete walls are chipping away, the girders of the old steel truss bridge holding fast but rusting and flaking, and below there is the muddy, rushing, angry Tar River, the depth varying by time of year. It seemed high that last time in late winter. There are falls below, one of several on the snaking river that meanders through Nash County and several others until it joins its sibling the Pamlico and together they press on to the Atlantic Ocean.

Across the river is Webb's Mill, once a thriving part of the community, was for years a place protected on the other side by chains across the driveway, keep out signs, and rough characters who appeared out of nowhere one day when I tried to photograph the mill, warning that I needed to take my ass out of there while I could and put that damn camera up. I was sure at the time some shady transactions went on there, off the beaten path. Maybe it's the river, swirling, foaming, it's greenish-cow turd brown waters, narrow, powerful through this part of the state, winding and unwinding so much so that just a twist and turn around the corner is yet another bridge to cross and where two additional bridges can be seen, both of them also abandoned. According to some of the oldest maps going back to the 1700s, an Indian path/trade route that ran from Petersburg, Virginia to

Fayetteville, North Carolina cut right through here. No traffic has crossed this bridge in at least four decades, but it stands strong against the clamoring, rushing current below. Someone was going to develop Webb's Mill into a restaurant back in the early 1990s with grand plans printed in the newspaper, but it never happened. I made scenic photos for a brochure for the Spring Hope Chamber of Commerce half a decade later, but not much came of it. There is good farmland and in some places, arrowhead rich hunting grounds, although I've never had much luck. Recently, new owners took over the mill and are using the property for weddings and music events.

I love the character of this old bridge, one that they don't seem to build or save in this style anymore. When I was a child, I can remember holding my breath when we crossed it in my daddy's pickup truck, the span so slight that a peek out the window showed a straight drop down, the road so narrow that if another vehicle was on the other side at the same time, Daddy would wait or they would wait, one car at the time, for width and load's sake. Once we were across, it meant a trip inside the old mill, dark and scary like the river, full of old men laughing and telling stories, but I didn't care or pay attention to what they were saying, I just watched the wheel spin and the stones turn while feed was loaded and maybe Daddy picked up a bag of cornmeal for his favorite fried cornbread that Mama made just about every night. Daddy grew up right across what is now a divided highway and always mentioned how he used to jump off the bridge when he was a boy, especially when he noticed my anxiety of us crossing. I would look at him with my mouth open, not sure whether to believe him, but if Mama was with us, she'd say, yeah he did and maybe that's what wrong with him now. We'd laugh, and I'd crawl around in the seat, between them, looking through the back glass as the old bridge disappeared around the crook in the road.

• • •

Writers write romantically about many rivers — it's easy to find in literature. Many waters in North Carolina have bold names like the Cape Fear or Native American names like the Pamlico, Catawba, Waccamaw or the Neuse, or contrary names like the New. Sometimes they even sound poetic, like the French Broad or the Yadkin or the Roanoke. Sometimes people build houses along them. Some rivers in North Carolina seem wide and beautiful and offer places to canoe and kayak or boat and fish and do river things.

The Tar is not really one of those rivers. It is not a pretty body of water — instead, it is sort of like the muddy-headed stepchild of state waterways. The name comes from the days when the river was highly trafficked with commerce, mostly tar barges to transport the naval stores of tar, turpentine, and pitch for which North Carolina was known. Steamboats and barges plied it daily. The Tar doesn't even get to be autonomous, as it becomes the Pamlico River after it passes under the U.S. Highway 17 bridge at Washington on its central-east-north-southeast route to the ocean, eventually emptying into the Pamlico Sound, one of those places well-regarded by water lovers.

As it winds and turns through my county, it comes within a mile or so of where I live. It's always been a place of mystery for me and despite the name and the water, it has its own beauty. On our way to town, there's a sharp drop to Bryant's Bridge, as it's known on emergency service maps, but not by signs, and for a moment, a rider seems transported to the mountains while solidly in the state's Coastal Plain. There are bluffs and huge rocks in the water and mysterious side paths. One time, there was a rooster who roamed the area around the bridge and there have been turkeys and heron and other wildlife, but mostly now it's the incredible amount of trash people somehow feel compelled to pitch from their cars as they near the water.

It's also close to the Indian Hole, a whirlpool that took the lives of three sisters one hot July day in 1931, girls who lived in the house where I grew up. It was a tragedy that made newspapers across the country and broke the man who'd also lost a wife and child to the Spanish Influenza epidemic years before — his ghost was said to roam our house and farm looking for his daughters and people would often ask Mama if she'd seen Mr. Josh lately. I've heard others talk of the Elephant Hole on the river near Rocky Mount. One legend has it that there are whirlpools supposedly large enough swallow a pachyderm. More reliable sources say the spot is so named b when P. T. Barnum visited friends in the city, it's where the circus elephants cooled off.

In more recent years, the Tar proved deadly again, rising from its banks during Hurricane Floyd, sweeping away houses and people that weren't even banks dwellers, cresting from 24 to 30 feet over its normal depth, busting 500-year levels. When the waters finally receded near my house, strewn in ditches were stoves and refrigerators and enormous loads of trash, some pulled from homes upriver, but much pulled from the bottom, a river some see as so ugly they use it as a trash pit.

•   •   •

The Tar River runs 215 miles before it becomes the Pamlico, making it North Carolina's fourth largest river. It starts in Person County near Roxboro and runs through small towns like mine, Spring Hope, and other places like Louisburg, Tarboro, Rocky Mount, and Greenville. Before the Civil War, it was so busy that the state legislature appropriated funds for dams and locks, but not all of those projects came to pass. If one wanted to ride the river from the source to where it becomes the more brackish Pamlico, it would not be possible without having to portage. It first appeared on a map in 1733.

In 1784, the legislature ordered Pitt, Edgecombe, and Halifax counties to clear obstructions from the river and in 1816, the Tar River Navigation Company was formed to control the river from the source to Greenville, except for Fishing Creek. They capitalized the company at $75,000 and permitted charging tolls. However, true to North Carolina's heritage, stubborn people and stubborn elements put up obstacles. The river was difficult to manage and many people in that time were against internal improvements in the region, and many of the wealthy and powerful wanted things to stay the same. Lawsuits had to be filed to make investors meet their obligations and a lock and dam was authorized at Pippin's Falls for $3,100, but it was abandoned before it was completed. The Board of Improvements that managed it was defunct by 1834.

Ten rare mussels, three rare fish (the brook lamprey, the Roanoke bass, and the Carolina mudtom),two rare birds (the loggerhead shrike and the black vulture), and a rare amphibian (the Neuse River waterdog) call the Tar home. At its deepest point in non-flood times, the river is 26 feet deep. The trees and tannins make the water dark and murky.

• • •

Despite its proximity, we did not go to the river when I was a child. My brother Bill would sometimes put in his jon boat with a friend to fish. This was a source of great anxiety for Mama, who only had to look at the old graveyard on the other side of the tobacco barns where the three sisters were buried for a reminder of the dangers of the Tar River.

This put a healthy fear in me as a child. It didn't take much since the bridge near our house had wood rails and it was clear they were rotting. There was a weight limit sign, a not-to-exceed one or two tons. It seemed dangerous and people often remarked it would only take a driver to lose focus for a split second and they would surely drop the twenty or more feet into the coffee-colored water, with no hope of survival. The state eventually agreed and closed our road for almost two years while a new bridge with concrete barriers was put in and the underpinnings repaired. We had to detour across a bridge near Webb's Mill, one that didn't seem much more secure, to go anywhere north. Later, at another bridge close to the junior high school, someone built a house on stilts on a bluff. I saw it flood so many times that I'm not sure if anyone lives there now.

• • •

It wasn't unusual to see people fishing from Bryant's Bridge. It always seemed like a risky choice, but both banks were private property and anyone looking a fish dinner had to stay on the right of way. These fishermen were usually the older black men of the community, sometimes with ancient rod and reels, sometimes with cane poles. Even in high water times, it was a long way to the surface and I never once recall seeing a fish pulled from the waters and I often crossed that river four or more times a day.

Sometimes there were younger men emerging from just under the bridge or walking up from a path. They offered long stares, and I wondered what they were up to. The paths and trails, some big enough for vehicles, were well hidden from the road and drug transactions were often rumored to take place. At night, sometimes a car would be parked at the edge of the banks, just off the road and I didn't know at the time what they might be doing.

•   •   •

My brother Bill lives on the Tar River Reservoir in Rocky Mount. He has a dock on a canal just off the city water source that leads into an open body that is filled with boaters, skiers, jet skis, jon boats, fishermen, and day drinkers during the summer. It is the "prime part" of the river in this area. There is a company that offers tubing rides, canoeing, and kayaking in certain sections.

Man has learned to build in view of the river, but not on it. There has been little development along most of the river, but it seems to be happening gradually. I don't know if it is good or bad–I wonder what the impact will be given the lack of regard and care for the Tar. Some efforts are made each year by non-profit groups that hold clean up days that yield thousands of pounds of rubbish, barely making a dent in the pollution.

•   •   •

Weird things happen near the river. My sister was driving across the bridge one day when a stray dog was standing in the middle — she blew her horn and instead of running away, it leapt over the side, a bizarre suicide.

I've never understood the trash dumping. What makes people do this, have the instinct or desire to throw everything from beer bottles and cans to fast food bags to takeout trays near a water source that serves so many communities. Sometimes, the fishermen leave their trash — they of all people should understand what they are doing. I've seen microwaves and toasters and countless pairs of shoes left in the gap between the bridge rail and the highway as if a drop off for some passersby.

• • •

What do rivers mean in other places?

Some communities develop around rivers, make them a centerpiece, build communities, beckon tourists, draw attention to the scenic beauty and the wildlife.

The Tar is a relic in an area of relics, a place whose better days are upriver in the past, no more traffic, no more milling, much less farming, less fishing.

There have been whale bones and shark's teeth pulled from the Tar. It may be dirty water, but it is still moving water, something that has entranced and sustained man since the beginning of time.

What does the Tar mean? It's not revered. There is a Tackle the Tar obstacle course fundraising event, and Rocky Mount has developed the old mills in town into a multi-use complex. The Tar doesn't appear in many paintings, there aren't really fishing shacks on it, and I don't recall any photography expeditions, all things we sometimes see in more "showy" rivers. But it rolls on, dark and dangerous and intriguing and full of life, a different kind of beauty.

17

Number One Pork Chop Man

"I tell him you Number One Pork Chop Man!" Su said in her charming, and I think intentional broken accent. Everything she said sounded angry, even when she was joking. She then looked at me and cackled. Su was short and round and held the arm of a slightly hunched, lean man with leathery, lined skin who wore a white apron and white hat. He pointed at me and rattled off something in Chinese. With a serious look on his face, he nodded at me and grunted. He then spun on his heels and went back to the kitchen.

Su came over and put her arm around me and squeezed. "He like you," she said, and laughed again. A good foot taller, I pulled her close while balancing my plate that was piled high with steaming noodles, vegetables, and her husband's signature dish, Garlic Pork. "That man is a genius," I said, "and you're not too bad either."

Su was my Chinese godmother. At least that's what I called her. She fed me, tried to teach me a little Cantonese and how to use chopsticks, although I didn't do well with either.

China Inn was in a low-traffic shopping center in Rocky Mount, a city wedged between Raleigh and the Outer Banks of North Carolina. The restaurant was next door to a pet store, which of course invited plenty of jokes. In the 1980s, before the proliferation of buffet style and takeout Asian restaurants, China Inn was high-end dining. Everything was cliché red: the cushions in the high-back chairs, the vinyl booths, the doors, and the cloth napkins, leaving only white linen tablecloths and dark woodwork and murals for contrast. At least a half hour wait on Friday and Saturday nights was required for a table. In our area, it was about as exotic as an eatery got, and drew an interesting mix of businesspeople, professionals, farmers, retirees, and laborers.

Common dishes on Chinese menus everywhere such as Beef Szechuan and Sweet and Sour Pork, were prepared in uncommon ways. They sliced the beef piecrust thin, lightly spiced and tossed with green onions. They deep fried the pork until it puffed up like a cotton ball and served it with vegetables, fresh pineapple, and an extra-sweet sauce. Their food was a treat, not anything like the offerings of the "fast food" takeout places that have sprouted up in shopping centers everywhere like mushrooms after a spring rain. As times changed, buffets became the standard in the Chinese food business. China Inn eventually followed this path, first adding lunch, then later, weekend dinner buffets, but the food was never greasy or engulfed in MSG.

• • •

Chinese food made its way into America via San Francisco and the great influx of railroad workers in the 19th century. Dishes had to be adapted to American tastes and available ingredients. It is a well-known legend that the very Chinese-sounding dish "chop suey" was created from leftovers thrown together. Anything with a tomato sauce or even with broccoli has been Americanized, since tomatoes are a product of Native Americans and American broccoli differs greatly from that in China. Fortune cookies were invented in California.

Ironically, in an era of dining that places a premium on heritage and authentic ethnic foods, American palates might be grateful. I have a nephew who works all over Asia and he told me that most of the time when he orders Chinese food, it is swimming in grease. He often sees cats and dogs in cages tucked away in alleys and side streets next to eateries.

• • •

The food at China Inn was always hot and fresh, and the family who owned it only made going there more interesting. It was more than that, though. They would laugh and joke, and even sometimes bicker, but for that they would switch from English to Chinese. Su was a character. She always seemed to be skeptical of new customers, even to the point of being curt, turning her face into a scowl of mistrust when she dealt with the unfamiliar. But that all changed after a couple of visits — loyalty earned conversation. If she saw you coming from the parking lot, she'd have a table ready and your drinks on the way. If she saw you in Target or the grocery store, she would call you by whatever your regular order was, put her hands on her hips, and laugh.

For my wife and I, China Inn became our "go to" place. We went to China Inn to celebrate job promotions, the day we went into business for ourselves, birthdays, and eventually, we just headed there every Friday night. Friends and family often tagged along, and some nights there might be 20 of us. Su or her sister gave us the private back room. We always had a great time, and like a typical godmother, Su would chide us to eat more.

China Inn had signature dishes, with the same names you see everywhere, but something was always a little different, a little better. There was a variation of Kung Pao (no peanuts, ahead of the curve in food allergy service), General Tso's Chicken, and Hot and Sour Soup (which I swear cured winter head colds better than any prescription). The best was Garlic Pork — thinly sliced, marinated, bite-sized pieces of lightly fried tenderloin, tossed in a dark, sweet, garlic and red pepper glaze with onions. It wasn't even on the menu, but a special order for "insiders" only. On nights they didn't have the delicacy on the buffet, Su appeared out of nowhere, laughing, with a huge plate she delivered to our table, usually with a word about us not being disappointed. Sometimes, she slipped us a container to take home.

"Don't let Alan see the bag," Su would lean over and tell me, as if we slipping me contraband to sneak past her brother-in-law, who worked the register. "You know how he is."

• • •

There are plenty of theories about the dish General Tso's chicken. I've never been in a Chinese restaurant that didn't list it on the menu, and it tastes about the same everywhere.

It is believed the dish originated in Taiwan and was introduced in New York in the 1970s. There were many leaders named General Tso in Chinese military history, but others say they named it to honor Tso Tsung-tang, who crushed Muslim rebels and defeated the Russians in the late 1800s.

• • •

"Su," I asked one night, "Are all these recipes from your family? Do you ever miss China?"

"Not really," she said. "Just Hong Kong. Glad to be out of China. Garlic Pork recipe come from New York, not China. My husband make up."

One night, when our daughter Holly was about three, Su announced it was time for Holly to get a tour of the kitchen. We thought Holly would protest, as she was still shy, but went right along with Su, long brown curls bouncing along. After what seemed like an eternity, the two emerged from the double doors, Holly clinging to bags of goodies stuffed with rice, fortune cookies, chopsticks, chocolate pirouettes and candies. "She's the perfect baby," Su said, beaming as a proud godmother might.

• • •

We never thought about China Inn not being there. That is until one night when Su looked distraught.

"My brother-in-law is selling this place, moving back to Maryland," Su said, barely masking her resentment. It was obvious she was not happy about the decision, even though she said she and her husband would stay and work for the new owners.

We went back once or twice after the transition. It just wasn't the same. The waitresses argued about who had to wait which tables. The restaurant was not crowded. Su was furious. "Nobody wants to work. This not going to last," she told us.

• • •

There is a scene in the cult classic, "A Christmas Story," which runs on a cable network for 24-straight hours at Christmas every year that I can't watch without thinking of China Inn. Ralphie and the rest of the Parkers have their traditional Christmas turkey ruined when the neighbors' dogs ransack the kitchen and decimate the bird. The family heads out to find some place open on Christmas — it turns out to be The Chop Suey Palace.

The family orders the closest thing they can find to turkey on the menu, which is Peking Duck, with the head still intact. Everyone at the table stares at the somewhat unnerving scene. Then the proprietor whips the cleaver down and decapitates the bird, relieving the tension that quickly converts into giggles and laughter and allows the Parkers to finally let loose of all that Christmas tension and stress.

We never ordered Peking Duck and I don't know if it was even on the menu. China Inn was less about the food as time passed and more about being an event to look forward to all week, a time for family and friends, and mostly laughter. Su was often the cleaver, the catalyst for all that, always with a gruff staccato followed by a warm embrace.

• • •

Shortly after it was sold, China Inn was no more. Shuttered behind those big red doors were a lot of wonderful memories — college decisions, engagements, pregnancy announcements, promotions, teasing, plans and dreams were passed across those tables, right along with the soy sauce.

There was my best friend's knack for running a serving spoon into a stainless steel tray and managing to get nothing but meat, no vegetables, as he constructed his "fried plate," a second serving with a purpose. We relished how the other waitresses thought my nephew was my brother, which meant they also thought my oldest sister was my mom. We laughed at my three stick-thin nephews, who were told by Su they needed to "put some meat on 'dose bones!" We debated whether fried rice and lo mein were merely a distraction from the finer things on the buffet. We talked about plans for the future, some realized, some failed. We talked about loves lost, starting families, and never once did I consider that our time together and the place would ever cease to exist.

I'm glad we couldn't see the future, because it would not have made us savor the moment more, it would have made us feel we were on the clock, consider that time was slipping from us, that lives were being lived faster than we knew, and that our special group would eventually stop gathering. Those dinners were a rare time in life when taking something for granted made the world right.

Since then, we haven't had perfect Chinese food. We've been to Raleigh, Wilson, and another place in Rocky Mount that is a pretty good substitute. We tried Thai and Korean and Japanese, much of it quite good, but nothing just right. And never any Garlic Pork.

The space is now occupied by a barbecue joint and I've found myself asking was the food really that much better than anywhere else? Was the 1980s chic atmosphere part of the appeal? Am I simply imagining something to be better than it was, as our brains often do when an experience slowly morphs into a memory?

Or, was China Inn part of something, something about my family and those who took us into their world and made us their extended family, even though we had absolutely nothing in common? There are places to get good food and service, but there is no Su to make it just right, to look out for the Number One Pork Chop Man.

18
Take Me Out to the Ballgame

I have a friend who tells me that when he gets to the Harker's Island bridge, one of the few quiet places left on the North Carolina coast, he can feel his blood pressure drop. He swears that more than once he's pulled over and checked. I don't want to know if he's telling a stretcher or not. He's a natural storyteller and when he talks about the place, I want to go there, because I've been and that strip of land in the water surely has transportive properties. It's the salt air, the slower pace of people and traffic and talk, the natural beauty of sight and sound — all those things work together.

Our trips to see the local Class A minor league baseball Carolina Mudcats offers a similar experience. I get anxious as we pull across the gravel parking lot, following the motions of the orange vest-wearing teenagers or senior citizens pointing the way emphatically, as if I might stray and throw off the precision of a lot that will accommodate many more visitors than will actually show up on a given night. We're an eclectic group on this family outing: the college-age daughter, just along for the ride and whatever funny stories she might add to her journal for future short stories; the teenage sons, one who looks forward to the non-game distractions, like the radar gun and the other who will zoom in on game action and cheer like it's the bottom of the ninth from the first inning on. My wife likes baseball, but mostly loves being outside on a summer night. *Bull Durham* is one of our favorite movies to watch together. Me, I'm there for the game, but really for all of it, the person the marketing people are thinking about when they talk about selling the total experience.

The smells set the tone early, wafting out into the parking lot: a little smoke from the cookers, hot dogs, hamburgers, pretzels. As we get through the gates, there is a faint whiff of beer and Pepsi, the hint of peanut shells already strewn in the aisles by the early birds. It's a small park and the vendors don't work the seats like they do in the majors. We like to sit on a row that was originally set up for wheelchairs until that section was moved under the cover of the grandstand to offer more shade. It's prime foul ball territory and close to the home bullpen. There is plenty of legroom, as it's the last row of the lower level on the third base line, no one to have our legs pressed into in front and no one behind to worry about obstructing view or spilling something on us. There is the swack-swack-swack of the booth over our shoulders where one child or adult or teenager will hand over a couple of dollars to throw three baseballs at a tarp while a speed gun offers the result. When I first saw these booths at fairs as a teenager, a contestant was supposed to guess the speed of the third pitch and get within a mph or two to win a prize. Someone figured out that no one cared about the stuffed animals or water guns, people just want to know how fast they can throw a baseball, who in the group can bring it, who gets the bragging rights, what dad can offer a glimpse of his past athletic glory or what sister who can whip an underhand fastball harder than her baseball playing brother. It's a game of wonder and ego and fantasy, that's the prize. And when someone uncorks what looks like a terrific pitch and it registers 70 mph — pretty fast, really — it offers a perspective on the pros just a few feet away who are popping 95-99 regularly on the field. The common problem for pitchers at this level is control. Sometimes, like the fans, the players aren't sure where the ball is going either.

On a perfect night, where late spring is slipping into soft summer, before the brutal heat sets in, just past the chill of the lingering early months, twilight cuts across the scoreboard. The grass is green and plush and perfectly manicured in this old tobacco field. The sky is just-right blue like it is in all those prescription medicine ads on TV. People are talking, laughing, glad to be here, glad to be out, glad baseball is back. The umpires have yet to miss a call, and the bad guys haven't scored yet.

And a common dream connects everyone in this ballpark. The players, coaches, umpires, trainers, and staff want to make it to the majors. The kids think they can be just like these guys one day, imagining themselves waving that bat, going into that windup, making that long run and catch and throw from the left field corner. And the rest of us remember what it was like to have that dream and are we old enough to know it doesn't come true for many. But it's enough to sustain the dream for generations and make an enjoyable evening wondering who might beat the odds while having a good time in the process. It is one of those most common American dreams to be a ballplayer and when that plays itself out, to enjoy watching others chase it. The minors are more casual, closer to the game. The best souvenirs can't be bought, they are stray equipment — balls, sometimes even bats.

Baseball is pure Americana.

• • •

The Mudcats, a low-level farm team of the Milwaukee Brewers, are cheap fun as far as sports entertainment goes. Where we sit would cost hundreds in the majors, lists for about $8-10 and can usually be had for less during promotions or with a Groupon, sometimes for as little as $4 on a weeknight.

There are no Crash Davises here, but there might be some Nuke Lalooshes. Most of the players are straight out of high school or college. They know one way or the other they won't be here long — they'll get promoted or they'll be out of baseball unless they get hurt first.

The outcomes at this level are not as important as the individual performances. Is this reflective of life? In Little League and each level as a player moves along, it's all about teamwork, being a team player — but that's all the teamwork training we get. In the end, it's a player's individual performance alone that determines whether he is among the 1 percent of the 1 percent who makes it to the major leagues. A certain selfishness is required for success, which we fans seem to resent when we see it played out, although in our own lines of work we've certainly seen the same dynamic.

Tonight, the early innings move quickly, and the play is crisp and routine. I remember when this team moved here from Georgia back in the early 1990s when I was finishing college. They were the Double A club of the Pittsburgh Pirates, a member of the Southern League. Some players went straight from that level to the majors and people were nuts over pro baseball. Trading cards were hot at the time and there were always people at the game early and stayed late hunting autographs. There was usually a ticket line and games against teams with lots of hot prospects often sold out. The concession lines were long. The seating was temporary, not as nice as the current setup, and the thought lurked in the back of the locals' minds that this team could pack up and be gone in the middle of the night, which has happened more than a few times in sports. This is Zebulon, North Carolina, not where the team planned on moving — they were aiming for the much heavier populated Raleigh area, but the Durham Bulls invoked their territorial rights granted by Major League Baseball to prevent it. So, the owner looked at a map and picked a spot as close to the limit as possible, where two major highways converged with two state highways and bought a bottom land tobacco field. The team even marketed the park as Field of Dreams and it was true: they came when it was built.

Because the field is down in a bowl, the ball does not fly out of here. However, the original parent club Pittsburgh Pirates played a couple of exhibitions here and I saw Barry Bonds hit some balls in batting practice that sailed out of the park and might have crossed the road and ended up on the bypass — and that was years before he was accused of steroid use.

Affiliates changed over the years, and the team was connected to the Reds, Marlins, Rockies, and even the Braves for a season. Players like Hall of Famer Chipper Jones and Red Sox legend Tim Wakefield came through. But most of the players don't become household names.

• • •

I love the folklore of minor league baseball. I love the old stories, which is probably why I love *Bull Durham* so much, that and the fact that some of it was shot in nearby Wilson and Rocky Mount and Durham. Earlier in the

20th century, there were minor league teams in many decent sized towns across the state like the Rocky Mount Leafs and the Wilson Tobs (short for Tobacconists). There was even fiasco called the Rocky Mount Pines that went 24-114-1 to post the worst record in the history of minor league baseball in 1980. I never got to a game, but despite the futility, I probably would have loved it.

I started my writing career as a sportswriter and baseball was easily the game I enjoyed covering the most.

•   •   •

It's an early Saturday morning in April. It's already hot as I settle into a seat in the grandstand's shade while my sons head for the field at Five County Stadium. The Mudcats, like teams across the country, have teamed with Chevrolet for free one-day skills clinics.

Both of my boys are nervous. My oldest, 13, maybe more so than his younger brother. He's never played baseball. He knows by his age, most other boys have been playing nearly a decade. I feel some guilt about this as I put him in soccer, thinking his preschool personality would not tolerate standing around in an outfield for an hour and a half. I think he secretly would love to be a pitcher, but for now I can tell he just doesn't want to make a fool of himself in front of these pro ballplayers or even the total strangers he's grouped with. My youngest decided when we were watching all those games on TV while I recovered from a liver transplant he wanted to give baseball a shot, and even though he's just 11, he's already way behind.

The boys get tours of the bench and field and clubhouses in between stations for playing infield, outfield, pitching, and hitting. The players and coaches probably don't love giving up a weekend morning, but if that's the case, they mask it well. In the stands, I can hear instruction and encouragement and laughing.

I see Kent get down low and field his grounders at second base and make the throw to first with some snap on the ball. I remember playing that position in Little League and would have given anything to be on this perfect ball field at that age. I too would have been nervous, a late starter myself, saddled with thick glasses, slow feet, and reluctant parents. When Kent gets to the mound and goes into the windup, he lets his pitch go with all he's got. It's in the strike zone and I see him look around quickly trying to figure out where I am and if I saw it. I know I need to remember to tell him I did.

Lowell is all business. It's obvious he wants to make a good impression and learn something.

I realize that in just a few years, most of these Mudcats will be out of baseball. Only a few will advance, and out of those, it's a long shot for even one to make it to the major leagues, much less stick. Many more of them will be coaches or teachers or policemen or construction workers or anything but a pro baseball player. They'll never forget their shot and the life and what they dreamed about, but for now, that dream is still on and someone has to make it in this game of attrition and today, in mid-spring, it could still be them.

In a couple of hours, the boys come back off the field and line up for free hot dogs, chips, and a drink. Some players sit behind tables and sign autographs. On the way out, the boys get a wiffle bat and ball to take home and a ticket for that night's game. I stop at the box office and buy three more. It was a good morning and the talk in the car going home is fast and furious and excitement lingers about our return later in the evening.

•   •   •

Minor league games have great promos and some that can be taxing. Shirts and caps are great, cow bells can wear on you. Lowell combined his cowbell and a beloved Mudcat foam finger one night into quite a spectacle. He takes every play seriously, yelling and screaming, emotionally invested in the outcome with a passion. After an inning or two, we could tell other fans were amused and my wife was a little embarrassed and his siblings were shielding their faces with cupped hands. About halfway through the game, a man approached us, I figured to complain about the disturbance. I wondered how I was going to respond. He reached a bag of peanuts to my beleaguered wife and said, while tipping his head towards our son, "I feel like you deserve something."

•   •   •

Cliché or not, few things connect fathers and sons tighter than playing catch. There is a promotion now after select games where families can go on the field and throw the ball around.

•   •   •

I turned the ball over in my glove, a Rawlings Dave Winfield model, looking for the grip I'd seen on TV. I looked in at the target, went into my windup, and let the ball fly. WHAP — the thud of my ball hitting the strike zone, a soft, weathered Masonite door on an old tobacco barn — echoed across the yard. I went and picked up the ball and narrated in my head how things were playing out for the Boston Red Sox in the World Series. They hadn't won a series in over 60 years or so, so the stakes were large. I imagined myself throwing Nolan Ryan heat and then a curveball like Steve Carlton. Regardless of the pitch, I usually struck out the last batter of the game, or worst case, someone would hit a long fly ball that one of my buddies — in my imagination — tracked down against the wall at the last minute to preserve the win.

I didn't have anyone around where we lived to play with, so most afternoons right after school and before chores I was throwing strikes for the Red Sox or shooting threes with Larry Bird and the Celtics. Some would say it was odd that a farm boy in eastern North Carolina had such an affinity for Boston sports teams and I don't have an explanation exactly, other than my brother-in-law John was a lifelong Celtics fan.

For years, I continued to throw at that barn door where I'd marked off a strike zone for years. The elements and my consistency took their toll, and Daddy had warned me to not throw balls at the door. Playing options were limited and the great thing about the Masonite was that it was springy enough to shoot a fast ball back almost all the way to my mound. If I missed the strike zone, the concrete base created ground balls and there was always the roof to send high fly balls, about two or three stories high. I could throw hot liners off the homemade basketball backboard my brothers had built me. One day, I let loose and the ball hit the door with a wet-sounding THWACK and the ball disappeared. It went through the door and into the barn.

At once there was excitement — I had literally thrown a ball through a door. That had to be impressive on some level. The excitement soon gave way to worry as I'd also ruined the door on the barn, which was long retired, but now served as a storage building. It took a few days, but finally my daddy noticed. He was not happy and he let me know it. One day when I came home from school, the barn door had been covered over with a piece of corrugated tin and my first sports ban was instituted. I tried a couple of days when no one was around, the sound of a ball hitting the tin was sharp and it was obvious the dents couldn't be concealed. I was now mostly a basketball player.

I begged to stay up on Monday nights for Monday Night Baseball with Al Michaels and tried to make sure I was done with whatever chores for the Saturday afternoon Game of the Week, almost always called by Vin Scully and Joe Garagiola. These were the only two ways to watch games. Sometimes, I could pick up a game on Sundays on the radio, but that was usually just the Yankees, and I didn't last long.

I loved baseball cards and had a couple of friends who did as well. We conducted mega deals and sometimes three-way trades that involved lots of logistics. In this "pre-valuable" era, we sorted our cards by team and kept them together with rubber bands. Newer cards were desired because they had the most up-to-date stats. I still have my cards and collect with my sons now.

One summer, I wrote to several major league teams — not just the Red Sox, but any team with players I liked like George Brett and Mike Schmidt and Ryan and most of them responded with black and white photos or stickers. In the days before email, official team stationery in my mailbox was a big deal. I checked the box scores every day and loved the stats and trivia and history of the game. I dreamed of a day I could go to major league games.

• • •

There are still a lot of mistakes made in Class A ball. In reality, many of the players aren't much older than my sons and some are younger than my college student daughter. It's easy to forget that the game can be tough after watching lots of major league games where it all looks easy and smooth, throws are on target, pitches are located, contact is hard — Class A ball is not polished. That's part of the fun and charm.

Baseball is also a perfect southern sport — slow paced with room to be social. A nine-inning game takes over two hours to play, and the action comes in bursts. There is time to talk about the day's work or the next day's plans or a trip we should take. We can work out suppers and practice schedules and then, with little effort, be in tune to a ball sent to the gap or that extra loud popping leather when a reliever is brought in and the scoreboard speed gun says he's hitting 99 mph. Over the years, the Mudcats have become more fan friendly. When they first arrived and the newness meant they were always packed, it seemed less so. That was a couple of previous ownership groups ago. The players too, seem to have changed. In the early days, some seemed to not only find the media annoying but also the fans. Now, it's not unusual for players to toss foul balls or last outs into the seats to lucky and eager kids, especially those who were savvy enough to bring a glove.

I love basketball for the bursts and the emotion and the momentum swings. Hockey is constant edge-of-the-seat anticipation and tension and makes even the casual fan get a little crazy from time to time. Baseball isn't any of that. It's laid back, it has its drama, but most often the stage is set by a series of events, where a story is built.

If you'd told me when I was a child that I'd live in the same area but be within 15 minutes of a professional baseball team, I would have thought you were crazy. If you'd told me I wouldn't be there every night, I would have thought that was just as crazy. But time and weather and life and economics restrict how often we go.

I got some distance from the game over the years, but when my liver disease emerged in 2015, I reconnected. I was limited in what I could do and watching the games was a way I found to relax. The rhythms and timing and pace provided calm. There were new things to watch for like exit velocity and the speed displayed on screen of every pitch. There were some games that helped me sleep — some would call this a negative, but not for me. And the Red Sox were fun to watch.

Batters have hot and cold streaks. All pitchers throw hard. The game is hard. Crash Davis poetically pointed out the narrow margin between success and failure when he said, "You know what the difference between hitting .250 and .300 is? It's 25 hits. Twenty-five hits in 500 at-bats is 50 points, OK? There's six months in a season. That's about 25 weeks. That means if you get just one extra flare a week, just one, a gork, a ground ball — a ground ball with eyes! — you get a dying quail, just one more dying quail a week and you're in Yankee Stadium."

But maybe it was Susan Sarandon's Annie Savoy who summed up the game the best, via an American poet: "Walt Whitman once said, 'I see great things in baseball. It's our game. The American game. It will repair our losses and be a blessing to us.' You could look it up."

19

Storm Surge

Hurricane Floyd taught me that stop signs are a lot bigger than I first realized.

There is a photo in one of our albums of my wife standing next to a stop sign we pulled out of a ditch days after the storm when we could finally get out of our steam box of a house. She's three months pregnant and the sign towers over her, tall and solid so that it can withstand the bumps of unattentive drivers, collisions of drunks, and theft or damage attempts by thieves or vandals.

Floyd pulled it out of the ground like a tomato stake going into the soft April-showered ground and flung it across the road, among the pine trees he'd treated just as roughly.

My wife is trying to smile as she and I and a friend try to make the rounds and see what has happened to our neighbors. The Tar River is still high and in control of several bridges and neighbors and Department of Transportation workers have tried to clear trees off roads and power lines. We'd been without power for about three days and wondered how long it would take to get over the effects of the storm. It would take about another week before they restored power.

• • •

Each day we break the monotony by venturing out to see how far we can go in each direction, how many trees people have been able to chainsaw and move off the roadways, not waiting for help that may or may not come.

• • •

At home, I'm running a generator we bought at Lowe's the day before Floyd made landfall in North Carolina on September 7, 1999. We learned our lesson three years before when Hurricane Fran waylaid us, the most damage I can remember in our part of eastern North Carolina in my lifetime. She was just a warmup.

We are unable to run air conditioning and it is one of those Septembers that thinks it's August. In North Carolina, we get those. We have the windows open and a fan running and the TV going. There's no relief. I feel bad for Kristi who has suffered nausea, and all that comes early in a pregnancy (her first) and I'm overweight and we're both miserable and trying not to complain and make it worse for the other. We're in our newly built home and though neither of us say it, it comes up later that we both have given thanks that we had moved out of the mobile home where we lived the first seven years of our marriage. Hurricanes don't respect mobile homes any more than tornadoes do and we've seen images on TV of trailers and houses alike being splintered. Many in our part of the state have lost their lives or family members and as the days crawl by, many more will die in the flooding or lose homes as the Tar and other rivers crest.

News helicopters fly over Rocky Mount showing much of the city is underwater. It was nearly destroyed and 20 years later, the scars are still prevalent, the city still trying to come back. Many fled and never came back. Princeville, a tiny town near Tarboro was essentially completely submerged. It's a disaster most of us had never seen the likes of.

• • •

I saw a story on the TV about a couple that had been flooded and it showed their possessions washing away in a stream, right there in the yard. An open wedding album spun and turned and I recognized it—we'd photographed their wedding. Working with the album company and our lab, we helped a few folks get replacements before the job simply became overwhelming.

• • •

Days later we finally made it to Nashville, and I had to show my driver's license at a traffic stop and state that I needed to check on my studio. The officer let us pass. We drove down Barnes Street thinking "this isn't so bad." Kristi and I wondered aloud if the media had overblown the situation, almost two decades before "fake news" became a buzzword.

We park at the studio and walk around. It's pretty dry. We breathed a sigh of relief for our three-year-old photography and framing business that's really starting to grow. A policeman is at the stoplight as we look down Barnes. We walked up the street since the light isn't working — we guessed power lines are down, or maybe there was debris in the street. We'd never really thought about our section of Nashville being on a hill, but it is. The Courthouse and most of the town is elevated and then there is a downhill stretch that leads to the major highway bypass, U.S. 64. Everything seemed fine. Just fine.

We got to the corner of Barnes and Washington, the "main drag" in Nashville. To the right, downtown, nothing seemed out of place. Then we turned the corner and looked to our left.

It was all underwater. All of it. We stood there with our jaws slack.

"Oh my," Kristi finally says.

I stood there and even though I was a professional photographer, I didn't make a single photograph. I didn't even bring a camera, and this was long before everyone had a cellphone with a camera.

The huge signs for Hardee's and McDonald's were visible as are some rooftops. Someone had a jon boat out in what was a parking lot near a small creek, but was now a lake more than ten feet deep littered with power lines and whatever cars were parked and the contents of countless businesses.

We stared for a long time.

Years before, we almost put our business in one of the little strip centers that we cannot even make out now. We had power at the studio and so we slept on the concrete floor for days.

• • •

We live about a mile from the Tar River in southern Nash County. Our road is hilly, as it drops to the banks of the Tar and then rises alternately, giving the illusion of the mountains, especially in late fall or early spring when there is fog.

About an eighth of a mile from the bridge that connects us to the rest of the county, the flood waters lap. My brother's son has already been and tagged the high water mark on the road in orange spray paint. The entire bottom — a neighbor's cow pasture, many acres of crops, all underwater. This seems to offer an answer why more people haven't built on the banks, given what seems like a love of waterfront living in this state.

• • •

We live on part of the farm that my family has owned since the 1950s. When Floyd hit, one of my brothers and one of my sisters each had homes across the road, and next door is my parents.

We all feel blessed, lucky, to have escaped major personal damage. We've lost some shingles, some small pieces of vinyl siding, and a couple of young trees.

Most of our plantings are new, our yard having been a soybean field less than a decade before.

My parents weren't so lucky. Their home had long been cradled by three old pecan trees, each believed to be over a hundred years old each that shaded three generations over their lifetime. They provided nuts and a place to play during my childhood. One held a hammock. The other, in the front, offered roots that could support small ramps for my bike when I was a kid and many battlefields for my green army men. Sixty years before, they shaded mourners for the three girls who drowned in the river on a hot summer day, trying to cool themselves in the Tar. Just years before that, they had held another service under that tree for their mother and baby, taken at Christmas in the second outbreak of Spanish influenza. The tree was protection from the road, the sun, and whatever else came down.

Fran took that tree leaving a crater the size of a swimming pool. Floyd did the same to one in the back, leaving just one tree and transforming the landscape of this previously quiet, safe place.

• • •

The New Orleans hurricane was more famous and Florida storms are more frequent, but the devastation is all the same for people who happen to be at ground zero of any storm. The pictures and stories soften even the hardest heart.

One thing I learned is that you never understand a disaster seen on television until it comes to you. There isn't just an economic toll, there is a physical and mental damage. My mama is elderly and got a generator that comes on automatically when the power goes out and it has served her well in hurricanes and ice storms since. But losing those trees were the passing of an era, when she and my dad bought this once raw place. If nothing else, it shows things don't stay the same, even if they've been there a hundred years. Anything can change and usually does.

For me, it was a loss of security from threats, that the one safe place, home, was vulnerable in a way I'd never seen.

20
Memory Cards

I studied the musky, fresh soil I'd turned out of the hole. I'd dug deep enough with the shovel, pulled out the roots of the previous failed effort, and paused to think. The sun was setting low over the high fields and the pond across the road, the end of another long hot day, the air filled with mosquitos. It would be dark soon, but I was determined to get this weeping willow sapling off to a good start. It didn't look like much, but I knew one day it would be spectacular. Three times as tall as me, the green, stringy branches would arch over and bend, perhaps around the time I might do the same.

We'd mark time and memories together, although I knew even as I carefully removed the nursery pot from the fragile roots, placed the tree into the hole and slowly broke up clods of coffee-colored loam, it would outlast me.

I must have looked puzzled with my task. In this particular spot of the yard, not long removed from a rotation of tobacco, corn, soybeans and cotton, I'd had trouble getting anything to grow. Just 10 feet away, blueberries and peaches flourished, as did a flowering cherry tree. But this spot was different. Hurricane Fran took out a promising red delicious apple tree, Hurricane Floyd swept away a honey sweet pear. The last occupant of the space had been a flowering shrub with red and white flowers, one given to us by my parents in sympathy. I don't recall its name.

My wife Kristi and I had talked about planting a weeping willow for years, and now I'd finally gotten around to it, an attempt to grant a wish just after we'd had another baby slip away. We'd suffered our second miscarriage just a few days after we'd seen the heartbeat on a black-and-white screen in the doctor's office. The hurt still burned inside like that late spring sun. I finished the job, put the shovel away, and went inside, satisfied with my memorial.

• • •

It took nearly three and a half years to close our photography studio and frame shop, and then only because we found someone who wanted to rent our 101-year-old building smack-dab in the center of the county seat.

I sold some of my equipment to other photographers, things like backgrounds and studio lights and props. Some things I could not part with, particularly the things that had become part of me and things I knew would never have the priority to be replaced, things I'd carried that I'd regret letting go the minute they walked out the door tucked under someone else's arm. There was my Canon 5D camera, a relic by digital standards, but still clicking along and a host of lenses, free of dings or scratches. These tools were the best, well-made and cared for as any craftsman or artist protects the instruments that allow him to tell the story only he can tell. My tools went home with me.

Unfortunately, many other items did too, including unsold frames, albums, and nearly two decades' worth of customer files. These files were filled with negatives from the first eight years and DVDs from the last nine years.

After all these boxes and awkward sized items took over our home, I started grabbing one box a week with the intention of methodically finding a place for everything. Eight years later, I still have remainders.

• • •

I always said that people think when they see baby smiles they are looking at mouths and teeth, but really they are looking at eyes. Eyes are always true to the heart, and that goes not just for little ones but adults. Body language is a close second.

· · ·

Rubbing against this impact was the change going on with me, and the constant, nagging feeling of *I just don't want to deal with this anymore*. I had become cynical and unsatisfied, questioned my purpose, even the value of what I was doing. Art on demand was what people wanted, not something beautifully crafted and designed to last. I was tired of crawling around on the floor, or out in the heat, stopping time for one moment, capturing one that should be enlarged to a 24x30 and placed on the wall of a home, only to see the client get cold feet when it was time to place the order. Weddings took most weekends and even print competitions had lost their fire.

I probably gave a dozen answers about why I closed the shop, and all of them were true, even though none of them were true. That's because my reasons changed. I changed. The photography, from both an artistic and business perspective, didn't change with me.

Some people spend lifetimes in newspapers, public relations or running their own business. Most self-employed people don't voluntarily shut themselves down to go try something new, jump into the unknown clutching a family of five.

But then again, I'd never really done anything anyone expected me to. I was bored and underpaid, and I figured I could change at least one of those.

· · ·

The weeping willow did not make it. I watered it each day, but slowly the green turned to brown, the soft, pliable branches into brittle brown sticks that resembled the fingers of a rudimentary Halloween witch. Grass mostly filled the area in, and soon there was no evidence the ground had been encroached on. I vowed to give up.

But I didn't. When our sons, who came along two and four years later, got old enough to ramble around the yard, they wanted to take pine saplings they'd gotten from the Smokey the Bear booth at the State Fair and plant them somewhere special. That seemed like a good idea, since pines in our area will grow in anything, whether it be a hole in a brick, rich soil, or red-orange clay. The pines failed, too.

A friend and client gave me one of the cypress trees he had been transplanting and having success within the county, a variety he had brought back from around the Pamlico Sound, where he owns a vacation home. He was very specific on the location, the soil type, how much sunlight and how much shade was needed. It was as if this tree was made to go in my yard; it was a place the tree could be good and different.

I once again armed myself with the shovel and a small trowel, and even brought along a measuring tape to get the depth and width just right. I used the large pot as a guide, remixed the soil in the bottom of the hole to make sure the roots could spread out. I watered meticulously, and it seemed at last there might be something going on, the best fit I'd been able to find. Then one day, while I was gone, the fellow who used to cut our grass wasn't watching where he was going and loped the tree down about an inch from the ground. It couldn't recover.

Nothing would grow in this space, nothing was quite the right fit, no matter what we tried. That bit of ground looks and seems very much like all that is around it, but it still waits to receive what is just right, what will live and grow.

21
On Being Country

"That is the most country thing I've heard you say."

A new poet friend I'd met at a writer's retreat told me this. She quickly clarified that she didn't mean it in an offensive way. I laughed.

I've been given the country or southern or Carolina label more than a few times, and I can't even remember the specific thing I said that morning that triggered it. She apologized because it is usually meant as an insult to be called country, although I usually say "thank you," because I don't think it is. Apparently, I say a lot of country things, Southern things, eastern North Carolina things. Honestly, I don't think people who are truly country would claim me and rednecks would say I'm not qualified. However, all native Southerners have a touch of it and can never shed it completely. Everybody knows the old expression: you can take the boy out of the country, but you can't take the country out of the boy.

Redneck has had a lot of meanings over time. It once referred to the necks of farmers who worked in the sun all day. Then it meant crass, uneducated, poor, rural white people from the South. Some added "inbred" to that, some added "bigoted," but for most of my life, it was always meant in a derogatory way, like "white trash" or "cracker" and could even be considered a racial slur depending on context. Jeff Foxworthy turned the insult into a comedy career in the 1990s, and now its arguable if redneck is even an affront. Most of the rednecks I know don't consider it to be one any longer, as now it seems to mean white males who like to hunt and fish and chew and drink and wear boots and expensive brand name clothing. It's a sort of a country version of a hipster that sometimes involves a lifted truck, a modified muffler and a Yeti cooler. Rednecks don't try to contain their politics or opinions, but really, these days, does anyone? Rednecks are almost always country, but you can be country without being a redneck — it's a fine line.

When I was a teenager, being from the farm or being country didn't necessarily make a person a redneck, having the added characteristic of being an idiot did — constantly wearing out tires, always wanting to fight, and getting in loud public arguments with their significant others were among the qualifications.

Country is someone who lives in the country or used to and wishes they still did. Country usually means the person grew up on a farm, or at least in a rural area. Where rednecks are often — incorrectly — assumed to be uneducated, that's not necessarily the case with country. Someone that's country might have multiple degrees and will probably get made fun of when discussing literature. Or they might not have a college education, but can build a house or fix a car as if they were born to do it. Some country people are also rednecks. Most rednecks or country folks have conservative beliefs or values, but not necessarily politics — for example, the Southern gentleman will open and hold doors for ladies, not because he feels they are weak or fragile, but because he was taught to respect women and to be courteous. It is not an offensive act, although, as I found out, it can be interpreted that way as I've been both scolded and cursed at for holding doors for women in public places. I've made the distinction here between "ladies" and "women" based on the language used in those episodes. Country usually includes manners, and we don't appreciate suggestions to go do something un-natural.

Country can mean, but is not necessarily, simple, honest, trusting, trustworthy. It usually means hardworking, although that isn't always clear because country can also mean a different pace in doing things, a thoroughness camouflaged by calmness or what some might describe as slow. This is sometimes confused with laziness or drunkenness, which may or may not crossover with redneck. The distinction can be made if you ask a person what their plans are for the weekend and they say "drinkin'."

There are other terms such as hillbilly that are often confused with country or redneck, but a hillbilly is someone from the mountains or hills, usually Appalachia (that's Appa-latch-ah, not Appa-lay-shuh). A hick or yokel is someone from the country who is unintelligent, and a bumpkin is naïve. Backwater can be a person or place that is remote in location or intelligence. Cracker used to be similar to redneck or a racial slur by other races directed at white people. Dirt farmer and trailer park are self explanatory, but also stereotypes far from the truth. Farmers are basically scientists without the Latin words. Deliverance, mouth-breather, and dumbass... well, they sort of go without saying.

The bottom line is that redneck and country are both used by non-red necks and non-country people as insults, but aren't always received that way.

I had a department chair once and a student who liked to "correct" or point out the Southern conversational colloquialisms spoken around them. I didn't much care for this, because honestly, correcting another adult's speech is rude outside of English class. I'm not sure where the professor was originally from, and even though he'd lived in the South a good while, he seemed to feel as though he was a cut above those in the surrounding community, both educationally and in taste. The student? He was a Yankee of sorts, having spent some time up North, but carrying that chip on his shoulder that so many Southerners resent, that "you're all a bunch of hick hillbillies around here, and back where I'm from we're all smart and classy and clever." Obnoxious persons verbalize this, and their smugness is complete when the Southerner declines answer, but is thinking, "hicks and hillbillies are not the same thing, and if everything was so great where you're from, why are you here?" Note: rednecks would sprinkle profanity among those words, and most likely add "ass" somewhere. As in, "Well, take your ass back, then."

The differences in Northern and Southern accents was broken down to me years ago: Northerners talk fast and drag letters, Southerners talk slower and drop letters. But this isn't always a North-South thing, when it comes to drawl, it is often a city-country conflict. Who gets to say which is better?

I remember being told as a young Communications major I needed to lose my Southern accent. I didn't need to change it, I needed to get rid of it by clearly enunciating words until no one could tell where I was from. Even then I thought this was terrible advice. No one should be ashamed or try to hide where they are from. They should hold on to their culture and heritage. That doesn't mean misusing or abusing the English language, but how boring would life be if we all sounded the same? Honestly, I love a good Tennessee accent, and a Boston one, too. I love talking to Texans and people from northern Virginia and Pennsylvania. I tell my students that talking and writing are two different things, and that as we get more comfortable in a conversation, we let our guard down, and out come the imperfections, and that's okay. I like it when they tell me, "You don't sound like a college professor," because I will do whatever it takes to make them understand what I'm teaching. When writing, we clean that up and be consistent.

For example, I've been known to drop the phrase "might could." I've heard and used it all my life and I didn't come to teaching until I was in my 40s. It is a phrase of hesitation used in an attempt to avoid being rude. For example, if there is an unwanted invitation at hand, or someone suggests a way to do something I know is wrong, or I see a solution to a problem that I really don't want to do, I'll use it. "I might could loan you the money." This means I don't want to, I'm not sure I'm going to, but I haven't said no, let me think about it. There's wiggle room. That's a few words used to express many, a major plus in communications, if not perfect English.

My wife Kristi is from the mountains of Virginia. My family and friends in North Carolina tease her because even after 30 years, she still pronounces phone as "fohn" and bone as "bohn" where everyone here sounds like "fawn" and "bawn." She sometimes even gets misidentified as a Yankee (anyone from above the Mason-Dixon line). She could qualify as hillbilly if she wanted, or country, or maybe even redneck — she's owned a truck and it was a stick shift. Conversely, the first time I went to visit her hometown, people seemed fascinated with the way I talked and wanted to me to say stuff for their amusement. And in North Carolina, we don't even think we have that much of a Southern drawl. Even now, when I go out of town to conferences or events where I speak or do interviews for stories, inevitably someone will say, "I love your North Carolina accent." That used to bother me, but now I take it as a compliment that I've held onto a sense of place — as long as they don't say "Carolina" when they mean "North Carolina." We just don't do that.

One of my favorite academics is a professor at North Carolina State University, Walt Wolfram. He's studied accents and dialects from all over, but especially in North Carolina and has a wonderful book called *Talkin' Tarheel*. There are QR codes in it that allow a reader to scan with a phone and hear words and phrases pronounced from different parts of the state.

To say I live in a rural area is an understatement. Growing up in the 1970s and 80s, more than one neighbor was without indoor plumbing. Our internet connection is a joke and high-speed access is as far-fetched as a flying car from *The Jetsons*. We used to joke that the electricity goes out every time a squirrel breaks wind. For most, there is only one provider choice for utilities, which certainly affects prices and quality.

But there is something to be said for living in a place where a point is reached in the day where there is no traffic, and a person can do whatever he or she wishes in his or her yard.

Education is a relative thing. A good mechanic or plumber or electrician is as appreciated — and sometimes as hard to find—as a computer technician, or car service or Uber to a city person. Fresh air is plentiful, food delivery is non-existent. The night sky is never corrupted by city lights, but there is a sense of isolation, especially in severe weather. We recycle stuff and sometimes it looks like white trash. Next-door neighbor means the closest person is about a football field away at least.

Being country means open spaces, fields and woods. It means no one is around much of the time, but there might be deer stands in those woods. Being country means being able to go to the bathroom outside. It might mean there's a fire pit, but there's almost certainly a burn pile, which balances out damage to the ozone by keeping things out of the landfill.

Culturally, there are drawbacks. Being country means being far from everything convenient and enriching—museums, concerts, theaters, and art galleries. It means you play basketball outside in all weather conditions and if you watch TV, you're usually doing something useful at the same time, like shelling peas. You make up for cultural activities by passing on the oral tradition of urban legends, folklore, and superstitions — cross your windshields when a black cat crosses in front of you, hang a dead snake on a fence post to end a drought, and crush your egg shells to keep the witches from using them as vehicles.

If I had to take a country or redneck citizenship test, I'd probably fail.

I don't hunt, and I don't like to fish. I don't drink, and I definitely don't chew tobacco. I don't like 99 percent of what's called "modern country music" and I don't drive a truck. I can't fix anything on my car more complicated than changing a flat, and that is always a challenge. I have no desire to be a farmer (again).

However, I can drive a truck or a tractor and a manual transmission. I like my guns and I like to shoot — targets, not animals. I am a conservationist. I don't like crowded spaces. My faith is important to me and so is the Constitution. I've farmed and tended livestock and respect farmers as much as any profession. I love bluegrass music.

I tried to learn to play the banjo and while I loved it, I was not very good at it. It is extremely difficult, and I took lessons, and tried to learn the guitar, and I'm not very good at that either. But I still try because it is fun.

I have no desire to go camping. I don't like to get dirty, but that could be as much a result of my liver transplant restrictions as anything — I'll stick with that story, anyway.

On snowy days, I've been known to get together with my neighbors (all family) and hook a kayak behind a four-wheel-drive truck to drag a person who apparently in that moment they climb into the kayak must self-identify as a hick to let someone drag them across acres of fields.

I know what chitlins and sause are and I'm smart enough to avoid eating both. I've eaten raw sweet potatoes, but I wouldn't recommend it. I love sweet potatoes cooked a hundred different ways, but sliced sweet potato pie is the best. Grits are good with something besides shrimp and are never eaten with sugar — only butter, salt, and pepper.

I've never lived anywhere that didn't have at least one basketball goal, and yes, I've seen people have knockdown/-drag outs — verbally and physically — over UNC/Duke/State basketball that have no ties to the schools other than they've always watched them play on TV, bless their hearts. College sports are serious business. Someone once unfriended me because I had the gall to post about East Carolina handily beating UNC in football.

There is a certain amount of "mouth" that comes with being country. At any point in an argument, someone might threaten to "kick your ass," used this way: "I'm going to come back later and kick your ass." The proper country response is — regardless of the size of the offender — "why wait?" At that point, chests inflate and chins elevate, and friends or associates are expected to step in and allow the potential combatants to save face while still appearing angry.

What's lost in those type things is made up for in the color of our language. Bless your heart, for example, might not mean what you think it does. My daddy often expressed his state of health by saying, "I feel like I've been shot at and missed and shit at and hit." Someone who is not very good at his/her job has "missed their calling." "Getting struck short" means having an unfortunate upset stomach in a social setting. "Come see us" is not an invitation just as "tell everybody we said hey" isn't expected to be taken literally.

Food has changed a bit. Pizza used to be limited to Chef-boy-ardee and the Inn or the Hut, but takeout has expanded those options. Mexican and Chinese restaurants have changed the food diversity. Country cooking still involves the liberal use of bacon grease, salt, and ham bones to flavor greens and other vegetables.

Country people are the original recyclers. Tires can be yard decorations, but it takes a redneck to paint them. Cinderblocks can hold a mailbox, frame a garden, be turned into a driveway entrance, or used to build a pig cooker. Old tire rims are almost as versatile.

Bluegrass will draw a country crowd and then there are crossovers like Lynyrd Skynyrd, who appeal to country folks and rednecks.

Not all country folks go to church, but the ones that don't know they should and feel guilty about it a couple of times a year, becoming CEOs — Christmas and Easter Only attendees. Country folks are not portrayed in flattering ways on TV because TV writers are rarely from the country, although ironically, many great and heralded writers of the past and present are.

Country people are strict believers in fair play and hard work, and don't often have money. However, they know the difference in being poor and not having money. And if they have money, they know not to show it. They are generally kind, bighearted and generous, which means sometimes they get taken advantage of and play into the stereotype of being ignorant or too trusting. They expect non-country people to treat them as they treat others and it often doesn't work that way.

Country people often pity people with too much book-sense, because those types often are limited in world skills. Country people pity white collar folks because they always seem stressed out. People from the country are survivors.

Of course, there is no one way to be country. A person can be partially country and the traits just don't go away, even though they might seem like it for an extended period. Country is never completely removed, not even over the course of generations.

There is less country to be country in now, and more people are covering their tracks. It doesn't show up on send-off DNA tests, but maybe it should. It's still okay to imitate a country accent, but frowned on to imitate a foreign accent — why is that?

In this age of emphasizing diversity, where someone is from should be celebrated as a tradition handed down for generations. Country is a state of mind and a culture and maybe that's worth trying.

About the Author

Michael K. Brantley is the author of four nonfiction books, including former Amazon No. 1 in Nonfiction and Memoir, *Memory Cards: Portraits from a Rural Journey*. He also wrote *Galvanized: The Odyssey of a Reluctant Carolina Confederate*, about his great-great-grandfather who served in both armies during the Civil War and was involved in a bizarre murder. Brantley has worked as an award-winning journalist and photographer and teaches English, Creative Writing, and Communications at Barton College. He lives on part of the former family farm with his wife and children in eastern North Carolina.

Note from the Author

Word-of-mouth is crucial for any author to succeed. If you enjoyed *A Southern Season*, please leave a review online—anywhere you are able. Even if it's just a sentence or two. It would make all the difference and would be very much appreciated.

Thanks!
Michael K. Brantley

We hope you enjoyed reading this title from:

www.blackrosewriting.com

Subscribe to our mailing list – *The Rosevine* – and receive **FREE** books, daily deals, and stay current with news about upcoming releases and our hottest authors.
Scan the QR code below to sign up.

Already a subscriber? Please accept a sincere thank you for being a fan of Black Rose Writing authors.

View other Black Rose Writing titles at www.blackrosewriting.com/books and use promo code **PRINT** to receive a **20% discount** when purchasing.

Lightning Source UK Ltd.
Milton Keynes UK
UKHW022312070223
416656UK00022B/269